Washington County Tennessee

SUPERIOR COURT OF LAW AND EQUITY

1791–1799

WPA RECORDS

Heritage Books
2024

HERITAGE BOOKS

AN IMPRINT OF HERITAGE BOOKS, INC.

Books, CDs, and more—Worldwide

For our listing of thousands of titles see our website
at
www.HeritageBooks.com

A Facsimile Reprint
Published 2024 by
HERITAGE BOOKS, INC.
Publishing Division
5810 Ruatan Street
Berwyn Heights, MD 20740

Reprinted
by
Mountain Press
Signal Mountain, Tennessee
2005

International Standard Book Number
Paperbound: 978-0-7884-8780-4

WASHINGTON COUNTY

MINUTES OF THE SUPERIOR COURT OF LAW & EQUITY
Feb. 1791 - August 1799

(p 141)   February Term 1791

At a Court of Equity began and held for the District of Washington within
the Territory of the United States of America South of the River Ohio in
the Court house of the County of Washington on Tuesday the fifteenth day
of February one thousand seven hundred & ninety one.
Present The Honorable

                 David Campbell)
                      &   (Esqrs.
                 John McNairy)

Andrew Russell produced a Commission, which is the words following to wit,
William Blount Governor "in and over the Territory of United States of America South of the River Ohio, To all who shall see these presents greetings:
        Know ye that I do appoint Andrew Russell of the County of Washington
in the said Territory Clerk and Master in Equity of the Superior for the
District of Washington and do authorize and impower him to execute and fulfil the duties of that office according to Law and to have and to hold the
said Office during his good behaviour or during the existence of the Temporary Government of the said Territory with all the priviledges and Emnul-
ments to the same of Right appertaining. Given under my hand and seal in
the said Territory this twenty seventh day of October in the year of Our
Lord One thousand seven hundred & ninety Signed Wm Blount By the Governor
Rich. Mitchel, with a certificate thereon that he had taken an Oath to support the Constitution of the United States and the Oath of Office.

Tuesday the 22d day of February 1791
        Present the Honbl David Campbell)
                      &   (Esquires Judges
                 John McNairy)

ALEXANDER HAMILTON - plt)
        against   (In Equity
JAMES PATTERSON ----deft)

                 (p 142) By consent of the parties by their Attor-
nies. It is Ordered that Commission issue to take the depositions of the
Witnesses in this cause on giving the adverse party thirty days previous
notice of the time and place of executing the Commissions to examine those
witnesses which reside out of the District, and ten days previous notice to
those who reside within the District.

JOHN WILLIAMS of Granville County Esquire

JAMES HOGG of ORANGE COUNTY Gentleman –
THOMAS HART of   COUNTY in the State
of Maryland Merchant and DAVID HART of
CASWELL COUNTY Gentleman plf
                against) In Equity
THE HEIRS and DEVISEES OF RICHARD HENDERSON
late of GRANVILLE COUNTY ESQUIRE deceased;
of NATHANIEL HART of   COUNTY IN VIRGINIA
Gentleman decd, of WILLIAM JOHNSTON late of
ORANGE COUNTY merchant decd, of JOHN LEETNAL
late of CHATHAM COUNTY Gentleman deceased and
LEONARD H. BULLOCK defts. JOHN UMSTEAD, SUSANNA
UMSTEAD, LEONARD H. BULLOCK, RICHARD HENDERSON,
one of the heirs and devisees of RICHARD HENDERSON
decd. A. HENDERSON, SYRICE MACOY, FANNY MACOY, JOHN
and ELIZABETH HENDERSON by SYRICE MACOY her Guardian having acknowledged the service of the Copy of the bill and
Subpoena in this Cause and they failing to appear and put in their answers
or pleas agreeable to the Rules in Chancery or demur; The said bill as to
them is taken for confessed and appointed to be heard exparte at the next
Court.

And the rest of the said heirs and Devisees not having entered their
appearance according to the rules of this Court and it appearing to the
satisfaction of the Court that they reside without the limits of this Territory. On the motion of the plts. by their Attorney it is Ordered (p 143)
that unless the said heirs & Devisees shall appear here on the first day of
the next term and answer the bill of the plts. that then it shall be taken
for confessed and that a copy of this Order be forthwith published in the
Cape Fare Gazette within sixty days from this time and in the News paper
regularly published in the District of Kentuckey for three weeks successively and at the door of the Court house in the Town of Jonesboro.

GEORGE MARTIN ---plt)
      against   (In Equity
ANDREW ENGLISH --deft)
                By consent of the parties by their Attornies It is Or-
dered that Commissions issue to examine and take the depositions of the witnesses in this cause giving the Opposite party ten days previous notice of
the time and place of executing the same.

WILLIAM NELSON ---------plt)
      against   (In Equity
JOHN HANNAH ------------deft)
                By consent of the parties by their attornies. It
is Ordered that Commissions issue to examine and take the depositions of the
Witnesses in this Cause giving the Opposite party twenty days previous notice
of the time and place of executing the same.

HENRY MASSINGAL ------- plt)
     against   (In Equity
DAVID HUGHS & JAMES STUART --- defts)

                                  By consent of the parties by their Attornies. It is ordered that Commissions issue to examine and take the depositions of the Witnesses in this Cause giving the opposite party ten days previous notice of the time and place of executing the same.

(p 144)   Thursday 24th February 1791.

        Present the same Judges as before.

SAMUEL BAUGHMAN ----------------------plt.)
     against   (In Equity
RACHEL DILLINGHAM & JOHN WOODS------defts.)

                                 By Consent of the parties by their Attornies. It is Ordered that Commissions issue to examine and take the depositions of the Witnesses in this Cause giving the Opposite party twenty days previous notice of the time and place of Exe auting the same, and that John Dunkam and George Vincent be commissioners for this purpose In Sullivan County; Henry Wood & George Sammons in the County of Greenville in South Carolina, and that Thomas Payne and Benjamin Ekles in the County of Washington in Georgia, and it is further Ordered that Rachel Dellingham the deft. give Security in the sum of One hundred pounds to abide by & perform the Decree of this Court.

WILLIAM BLEVINS & OTHERS ---plts)
        against   (In Equity
JOHN SHELBY ----------------defts)

WILLIAM BLEVINS & OTHERS----plts)
       against   (In Equity
JOHN SHELBY ---------------defts)

WILLIAM BLEVINS ----------- plts)
       against   (In Equity
JOHN BROWN ---------------defts)

JOHN SHELBY -----------plt)
       against   (In Equity
WILLIAM BLEVINS & OTHERS--defts)

(p 145)   DUE on the DEMISE OF JOHN SHELBY plt.)
               against   (In Eject. by Consent
           WILLIAM BLEVINS & OTHERS   )

On the Motion of John Shelby and John Brown defts. by their Attorney in the foregoing suits in Equity, It is ordered that Other Sufficient Security be given for the prosecution of the said suits in the sum of four hundred pounds and on the motion of the said Blevins & Others by their Attorney. It is Ordered that the said Shelby and Brown be bound in the sum of four hundred pounds Current money to abide by and perform the Decree of the court in the said suits. And by agreement of the parties by their Attornies the Jury of View in the Cause in Ejectment is discharged from their attendance until the eight day of the next term; that those depositions which have heretofore been taken by the parties on ten days notice shall never be excepted to by either party on account of not having longer notice and that Commissions shall issue to take the depositions of the rest of the Witnesses in these Causes on giving the adverse party legal notice of the time and place of exacting the same. and for reasons appearing to the Court. It is Ordered that these Causes be Continued till the next term.

SIMON KIRKENDOL ---------------plt)
     against   (In Equity
ROBERT MCAFEE ------------deft)

                   For reasons appearing to the Court, It is Ordered that this cause be continued till the next term.

DAVID MCPETERS and CHARLES MCDOWELL ----plts)
     against   (Equity
ALEXANDER OUTLAW,MARTIN CASWELL and   (
JOHN HERRITAGE -------------------------defts φ

(p 146) By consent of the parties by their attor. It is Ordered that this Cause be continued till the next term, and that Commissions issue to examine and take the depositions of the Witnesses in this Cause giving the adverse party legal notice of the time and place of executing the same.

JOHN ADAIR -----------------plt)
     against   (Equity
EDMUND WILLIAMS -----------deft)

                 By consent of the parties by their Attornies It is Ordered that this Cause be Continued till the next term.

JOHN AARONWINE -------------plt)
     against   (Equity
JOHN SHELBY ---------------deft)

                 By consent of the parties by their Attornies It is ordered that John Hackett a Surveyor for the plt. and Joseph Greer for the deft. attend and run out and Survey the lands in dispute agreeable to the bounds & lines expressed in each partys title and make three accurate plans of such Surveys and return the same to the next Court.

CHARLES HAYS -----------plt)
     against   (Equity
SAMUEL HARRIS --------deft)

              For reasons appearing to the Court. It is Ordered that this Cause be continued till next term and that a Commission issue on behalf of the deft to Burk County to examine and take the deposition of Witnesses in this Cause on giving the plt. legal notice of the time and place of executing the same.

(p 147)   GEORGE MARTIN ---------plt)
                    against   (Equity
             ANDREW ENGLISH -------deft)

             WILLIAM NELSON ------plt)
                    against   (Equity
             JOHN HANNAH --------deft)

For reasons appearing to the Court, It is Ordered that these Suits be cont^d. till the next Court and by Consent of the parties, It is agreed that no exceptions shall be taken to depositions heretofore taken on ten days previous notice.

JOHN TADLOCK -------------plt)
        against   (Equity
ISAAC RUTLAND ---------deft)

By Consent of the parties by their Attornies It is Ordered that this Cause be continued till the next term and that Commissions issue to examine and take the depositions of the Witnesses in this Cause giving the opposite party legal notice of the time and place of executing the same.

ALEXANDER HAMILTON ------plt)
        against   (Equity
JAMES PATTERSON ---------deft)

By consent of the parties, It is ordered that this Cause be continued till the next term, and that Other and better security be given by the plt. for the prosecution of this Cause.

HENRY WASSINGAL -------------plt   )
        against   (Equity
DAVID HUGHS & JAMES STUART--defts)

By consent of the parties by their Attornies, It is Ordered that this (p 148) cause be continued till the next term and that Francis A. Ramsey a surveyor for the deft. and Joseph Greer a Surveyor for the plt. attend and run out and Survey the lands in dispute agreeable to the lines and bounds expressed in each partys title and make three accurate plans of such Surveys and return the same to the next Court.

RUTH BROWN -----plt.)
    against   (Injunction in Equity
JOHN McDOWELL ---deft.)

For reasons appearing to the Court. It is Ordered thatthis Bill of Injunction be dismissed

JOHN BULL ------------plt)
    against   (Equity
BENJAMIN GOODWIN-----deft)

James Stinson deputy Sheriff of Greene County having made affadavit that he served the deft. with a copy of the bill and taken his body out on a writ of Capias in proper time and he failing to appear and put in his answer on plea agreeable to the rules in Chancery or demur; the said Bill is therefore taken for confessed and appointed to be heard ex-parte at the next term.

JOHN WADDEL ----------plt.)
       against   (Equity
ROBT. PATTERSON -----deft.)

                Time is given the deft. till next term to put in his answer.

                         David Campbell, J. T. W. S.
                         John McNairy, J. T. W. S. S. R. A.

(p 149)   At a Court of Equity Begun and held at the Court house in Jonesborough the 15th day of August 1791 for the District of Washington in the Territory of the United States South of the River Ohio.
   Present the Hon^{bl} David Campbell) Esqr.
                     &   (
          Joseph Anderson) Judges

JOHN TADLOCK -----------Compt.)
       agst.   (On a Injunction in Chancery
ISAAC BULLARD ----------Deft.)

                By Consent of the parties, It is Ordered that this suit be dismissed at the Costs of the Complt. the deft having previously acknowledged Satisfaction for the Debt mentioned in the Complts. Bill.

            Andrew Russill Clerk and Master in Equity entered into and acknowledged his Bond according to Law which Bond is in the words following to wit:

Know all men by these presents that Andrew Russell Alexander Outlaw John Rhea and Joseph Love -----------are held and firmly bound unto the honorable David Campbell John McNairy and Joseph Anderson Esquires Judges in and over the Territory of the United States South of the River Ohio, and to their Successors in Office in the sum of Two Thousand pounds current money; To the payment whereof to be made to the said Judges and their successors in office we bind Ourselves our heirs executors and administrators jointly and severally firmly by these presents, sealed with our seals and dated this 23rd day of August 1791.

The Condition of the above obligation is such that whereas the above bound Andrew Russell hath been constituted and appointed Clerk and Master in Equity for the District of Washington in the Territory by Commission from his Excellency William Blount Esqr. bearing date the 27th (p 150) day of October 1790 If therefore the said Andrew Russell shall safely keep the Records of the Court of Equity for the said District of Washington and shall faithfully discharge his duty in Office then the above obligation to be void Otherwise to remain in full force and Virtue. Andrew Russell L. S. Alexr. Outlaw (L. S.) John Rhea (L.S.) Josiah Love (L. S.)

RICHARD BRINDLE ------Complainant)
      agst.   (on an Injunction
CALEB CARTER --------Defendant)

                    The Attorney for the Complainant having produced an Order signed by the Deft and attested by two witnesses directing this suit to be dismissed at his Costs. For those reasons It is Ordered by the Court accordingly.

SIMON KIRKYNDOLL ----------Complainant)
      against   (Injunction
ROBERT MCAFFEE ----------Deft.)

                For reasons appearing to the Court It is Ordered that this cause be continued till next Term.

DAVID MCPETERS and CHARLES MCDOWELL -Complt)
      agst   (Chancery
ALEXANDER OUTLAW MARTIN CASWELL (
and JOHN HERRITAGE -----------------Defts)

                For reasons appearing to the Court It is Ordered that this Cause be continued till the next term.

JOHN WADDEL --------------Complt.)
      agst.   (Equity
ROBERT PATTERSON ------ deft.)

                Time is given the deft. till next November Court to put in his answer.

(p 151)   JOHN ADAIR --------Complt)
         against   (Injunction
        EDMUND WILLIAMS ---Deft.)

                For reasons appearing to the Court It is Ordered that this Cause be continued till next term. And it is ordered that Commissions be awarded the parties to examine and take the depositions of the Witnesses in this Cause giving legal notice of the time and place of executing the same.

JOHN AARGWIRE -------Complainant)
      against   (Equity
JOHN SHELBY ------------Defendant)

                For reasons appearing to the Court It is Ordered that this Cause be continued till the next, and that Commissions be awarded the parties to examine and take the depositions of the Witnesses in this cause on giving legal notice of the time and place of executing the same.

CHARLES HAYS ------Complainant)
      agst   (
SAMUEL HARRIS -----Defendant)

                For reasons appearing to the Court, It is Ordered that this cause be Continued till the next term, and that Commissions be awarded to the parties to examine and take the depositions of the

Witnesses in this Cause on giving legal notice of the time and place of executing the same, Cmplts. notice to the defts Attorney to be sufficient.

SAMUEL BAUGHMAN ------ Complt   )
        against   (Equity
VACHEL DELLINGHAM & JOHN WOOD -- defts)

                          By consent of the parties by their Attornies It is ordered that this (p 152) cause be dismissed at the Costs of the Complainant.

WILLIAM BLEVINS ------Complainant)
        against   (Equity
JOHN BROWN ---------- deft   )

                          By consent of the parties by their attorneys It is Ordered that the probat of the defts. answer be Sufficient.

ALEXANDER HAMILTON ----Complainant)
        against   (Equity
JAMES PATTERSON -------Deft.   )

                          The Deft having departed this life since the Commencement of this suit. It is Ordered that the same be abated and that a Scire facias issue against the executors or administrators of the said decedant, to revive the said suit.

WILLIAM NELSON ------Complainant)
      against   (Equity
JOHN HANNAH --------Defendant   )

                          For reasons appearing to the Court, It is Ordered that this cause be continued till next term.

HENRY MASSINGAL --------Complainant)
        against   (Equity
DAVID HUGHS and JAMES STUART --Defts)

                          By consent of the parties by their attorneys It is Ordered that this cause be continued till the next term, and that commissions are awarded the parties to examine and take the depositions of the Witnesses in this cause giving legal notice of the time and place of executing the same. And it is Ordered that Joseph Greer a Surveyor for the Complainant and Francis Alexander Ramsey a Surveyor for the deft run out and Survey the lands in dispute agreeable to the (p 153) lines and bounds expressed in each partys Title and make three accurate plans of such Surveys and return the same to the next Court.

DAVID MCPETERS and CHARLES MCDOWELL---Complts)
          agst.   (Equity
ALEXANDER OUTLAW, JOHN HERRITAGE and   (
MARTIN CASWELL   --- defts)

                          For reasons appearing to the Court It is Ordered that Jas. Galbreath Surveyor for plts F. A. Ramsey for defts. run out and Survey the lands in dispute included in the Grant Obtained by John Herritage for six hundred and forty Acres in Greene County on the

North side of Nola Chucky joining Martin Caswell including the mouth of
Flat Creek and one other by Martin Caswell for the same quantity on the
North side of Nonachucky Joining an Entry made in the name of Pharoah
Cobb.

```
WILLIAM COX ----------------Complt )
          agst                     ( Equity
AUGUSTINE BRUMLEY ----------Deft. )
```
                                   By consent of the parties It is order-
ed that this Cause be continued till next Court and that Commissions be
awarded the parties to examine and take the depositions of the witnesses
giving legal notice of the time and place of executing the same.

```
JOHN WILLIAMS ESQUIRE of GRANVILLE COUNTY
JAMES HOGG of ORANGE COUNTY Gentleman
THOMAS HART of ------COUNTY in the STATE
of MARYLAND MERCHANT and DAVID HART of
CASWELL COUNTY Gentlemen ---------Complts
          against ) Equity
THE HEIRS AND DEVISEES of RICHARD HENDERSON
late of GRANVILLE COUNTY ESQRS. deceased of
NATHANIEL HART of --------COUNTY IN VIRGINIA
Gentlemen decd. (p 154)  of WILLIAM JOHNSTON
late of ORANGE COUNTY Merchant decd. of JOHN
LUTTERAL of CHATHAM COUNTY Gentleman decd. &
LEONARD H. BULLOCK ---------------------Defts
```

Some of the said Heirs and Devisees having failed to enter their appearance
according to the Rules of this Court and it appearing to the satisfaction
of the Court that they reside without the limits of this Territory on the
motion of the Complts by their Attorney It is ordered that unless the said
heirs and Devisees shall appear here on the first day of the next term and
answer the bill of the Complainants that then it shall be taken for confess
ed, and that a copy of this order be forth with inserted in the Cape Fear
Gazetts the Kentuckey Gazette and Knoxville Gazette and the newspaper regularly published in Hagerstown for three weeks successively and at the door
of the Court house in the Town of Jonesboro

```
GEORGE MARTIN ----------Complt )
          against              ( Equity
ANDREW ENGLISH --------- deft. )
```
                                   For reasons appearing to the court It is
ordered that Other Sufficient security be given for the prosecution of this
suit.

```
WILLIAM BLEVINS and OTHERS -----Complts.)
          against                        ( Equity
JOHN SHELBY ----------------------Deft  )
```
                                   This day came the parties by their
attornies and thereupon came also a Jury to wit, Joseph Britton, Landon Car
ter, Joseph Conway, Henry Conway, William Conway, John Sevier, William Trem
ble, John Blair, Jessee Hoskins, William Horner, Asahel Rollings & Wyat

Stubblefield who being sworn well and truly to enquire "whether the lands in dispute between the parties were ever known to be in the County of (p 155) "Augusta in the State of Virginia" upon their oath as say that the land in dispute never Lay in the State of Virginia in the County of Augusta and the aforesaid Jurors being sworn well and truly to enquire whether the Government of Virginia did exercise or assume Jurisdiction on the North side "of the Holstein including the lands in dispute between the parties at the time of the Grant in the year 1753 & from that time until the extending the line in 1799 or at any time during that period" upon their oath do say that the Government of Virginia did assume & exercise Jurisdiction on the North side of the Holstein including the lands in dispute between the parties.

And the aforesaid Jurors being sworn well and truly to enquire whether the lands claimed by the complainants are those Covered by the old patent Grant under which the deft claims upon their Oath do say that the lands claimed by the Complts. are those covered by the old patent Grant under which the defts claim, and it is ordered that this Cause be continued till the next term and that Commissions be awarded the parties to examine & take the depositions of the witnesses in this Cause giving legal notice of the time and place of executing the same.

SAMUEL WILSON ------------------plt.   )
     agst   (Upon a motion for failing to execute
THOMAS BERRY SHERIFF of HAWKINS deft.) a process on E. Walden.

                           For reasons appearing to the Court it is Ordered that the deft. be fined fifty pounds Current money Nisi Ordered that notices to the attornies at Law for parties Litigent in this Court who reside without the limits of this Territory shall be good & legal notices.

SIMON KERKYNDOLL -----Complainant)
     against   (Equity
ROBERT MCAFFEE ---------deft/   )
                         For reasons appearing to the Court It is Ordered that unless the (p 156) said deft. shall appear here on the first day of the next term that then _____ Compls bill shall be taken for confessed, and it is Ordered that a copy of this Order be forth with inserted in the Knoxville Gazette (if any be published) for three weeks successivey and at the door of the Court house in Jonesboro

WILLIAM NELSON ----------Complt.)
     against   (Equity
JOHN HANNAH ------------deft   )
                      On the Motion of the parties by their Attornies It is ordered that Commissions be awarded them to examine and take the depositions of the Witnesses in this cause giving legal notice of the time and place of executing the same.

SAMUEL WILLSON ----------Complt)
     against   (Equity
ELISHA WALDEN ----------deft   )

The deft. having filed his plea in Abatement of the Complainants bill on argument whereof It is Ordered that the Complainants bill be dismissed at the Costs of the Complainana and it is Ordered that this suit ne cont'd as an Original Bill in Equity.

GEORGE MARTIN ----------Complt)
        agst.   (Equity
ANDREW ENGLISH ---------deft)

For reasons appearing to the Court It is Ordered that this cause be continued till the next Term and that Commissions be awarded the plt. to examine and take the depositions of the witnesses in this Cause giving legal notice of the time and place of executing the same, and the same for the deft according to the written application of his attorney & that notice to the Complts be sufficient.

(p 157)   JOHN BULL --------Complt)
        agst.   (Equity
        BENJAMIN GOODWIN---deft)

This cause was heard exparte upon the bill of the complt. which is in the words following "North Carolina Washington District Superior Court of Equity August term 1790" To the honorable the Judges of the Superior Court of Equity" on consideration whereof It is ordered and Decreed that the Several bills of Sale for the property of John Bull Complt. given to the deft. Benjamin Goodwin be annulled & made void for fraud practised by the said deft. in obtaining the same, that the said deft. be decreed to bring the said Bills of Sale into this Court to be annulled that the deft. restore to the said Complt the several articles of his property mentioned in the same Bill of sale and that the said deft. pay to the saidComplt the sum of four pounds thirteen shillings " four pence in restitution for the sum of three pounds ten shillings Virginia money fradulently obtained by the said deft of and from the Complt. on a false void & fradulent pretence of having an Entry for the improved Lands of the said Complt. in the Gap of Bays Mountain & that the Complt recover his Costs. And it is Ordered that an attachment be awarded agst. the deft. to enforce the foregoing Decree and it is further Ordered that a Scire facias issue agst. his Securetys.

DAVID MCPETERS & CHARLES MCDOWELL ------Complts)
            against   (Equity
ALEXANDER OUTLAW, JOHN HERRITAGE   (
and MARTIN CASWELL ----------------------defts)

On the motion of the defts. by their Attorneys It is Ordered that Other Sufficient Security be given for the prosecution of this suit. (p 158) And for reasons appearing to the Court It is ordered that unless the defts. John Herritage & the heirs of Martin Caswell shall appear here on the first day of the next term that then the bill of the Complts shall be taken for confessed and that a Copy of this Order be forthwith published in the Cape Fear Gazette & the Knoxville Gazette for four weeks successively and at the door of the court house in the town of Jonesboro.

Ordered that the Court be adjourned till Court in Course.

(p 159)   At a Court of Equity Begun and held in the town of Jonesborough the fifteenth day of February One thousand seven hundred and ninety two for the District of Washington in the Territory of the United States of America South of the River Ohio.
          Present the Honorable,

                              David Campbell)Esquires
                              Joseph Anderson(Judges
                              John McNairy   )

JAMES BRYANT ---------------------Complt)
          agst   (upon a writ of Inquisition
JAMES HOUSTON, ALEXANDER OUTLAW & the   (&
heirs of JOSEPH BULLARD decd --- Defts) Bill in Equity

                         on the motion of the defendants by their Council and
for reasons appearing to the Court It is Ordered that the Writs of Injunction Obtained by the Complainant against James Houston and the heirs of
Joseph Bullard decd to stay the Proceedings at Law mentioned in his Bill of
Complaint be dissolved and that the sd. defts. James Houston & their heirs
of Joseph Bullard decd recover the Costs. And on the motion of the Complain
ant by his Council It is Ordered that the Bill of Complaint exhibited in
this cause be continued as an Original Bill.

SAMUEL WILSON ----Plt)
      against   (Upon a Bill cont'd as an Original Bill by an Order
ELISHA WALDEN ----deft) of Court after the dissolution of the Writ of In-
                         junction.
                         By directions of the Plts. Attorney It is Ordered
that this suit be dismissed.

(p 160)   JOHN BULL -------Plt.   )
               agst.   (
        CALEB CARTER and ALEXANDER GOODWIN --Defts) Upon A writ of Scire
                                                     facias upon a Bond en
tered into By the said Defts. with Benjamin Goodwin the 25th day of October
1790 for the appearance of the said Benjamin Goodwin at the Suit of the Plt.
in Equity on the 25th day of February 1791 at the Court house in the Town of
Jonesborough.
             This day came the Plt. by his Attorney and the said deft. being
solemnly failed to appear; Thereupon It is considered by the Court that the
Plt. have execution against the said defts. for the sum of four pounds thirteen shillings and four pence the sum in the Decree Obtained by the Plt.
against the aforesaid Benjamin Goodwin at the last Term, and the Costs by him
expended in the Prosecution of his suit aforesaid here.

WILLIAM BLEVINS and OTHERS - Complts)
          agst   (Two Suits in Equity
JOHN SHELBY -------------------Defts)
                         For reasons appearing to the Court,
It is Ordered that these suits be continued till the next term, and that Publication of the Testimony be passed on the first day of May next - and on the
motion of deft by his Attorney. It is Ordered that a commission be awarded
him to examine and take the deposition of Mr. John Fowler in Kentucky on giv-

ing the Complts. thirty days previous notice of the time and place of executing the same - And on the motion of the Complts by their attorney It is
Ordered that Commission be awarded them to examine and take the depositions
of their witnesses in these suits giving the deft Legal notice of the time
and place of executing the same.

(p 161)   WILLIAM BLEVINS ----Complts)
                      agst   (Equity
        JOHN BROWN ----------Deft.   )

For reasons appearing to the
Court It is Ordered that this suit be continued till next term and that Commissions be awarded the parties to examine and take the depositions of the
witnesses in this cause giving the adverse party legal notice of the time and
place of executing the same, and that publication of Testimony be passed on
the first day of May next.

PETER MCCALL -------------Complt.)
         against   (In Equity
JOHN FAGAN -------------Deft.)

By consent of the parties by their Attornies
All matters in difference between them are referred to the determination of
Gilbert Christian, John Long, George Maxwell and Abraham McChallon and in case
of disagreement they are to choose & umpire whose award is to be made the Decree of this Court and the same is Ordered accordingly.

DAVID MCPETERS & CHARLES MCDOWELL -----Complts)
        agst.   (
JOHN HERRITAGE, MARTIN CASWELL and   (
ALEXANDER OUTLAW ------------------------defts)

The demurrer of the defts
Martin Caswell to the Bill of the Complainant being heard upon the argument
of the Counsel on both sides. It seems to the Court here that these Complts.
Bill and the subject matter therein contained are sufficient in Law for them
the said Complts to maintain their said Bill of Complaint against the said
deft. neither is he compelled to put in any further or other answer to the
same. Therefore it is con- (p 162) sidered by the Court that the Complts.
take nothing by their said Bill of Complaint but that the said deft. be hence
dismissed with his Costs by him about his defence in this behalf expended
and the Demurrer of John Herritage to the Bill of the Complts. being heard
upon the arguments of the Counsel on both sides being heard, It seems to the
Court here that the said Complts bill and the facts therein contained are
sufficient in Law for them the said Complts. to maintain their said Bill of
Complaint against the said deft. John Herritage and that he is Compelled
to put in a further answer thereto __ And on the prayer of the said deft.
John Herritage by his Counsel time is given him till the next term to put
in his answer. And on the motion of the parties Commissioners are awarded
them to examine and take the depositions of their witnesses on giving the
adverse party legal notice of the time & place of executing the same.

An Instrument of writing was exhibited in Court which is in the words following: Whereas Evan Shelby hath Bought the improvements and tract of Land of

John Cox where he now lives and if the Patents Granted to John Buchanan where Collo. Preston & William Campbell now executors for the said Buchanan estate and if the said Patent for the said should be broke or vicated and the said land to be vacant and no other elder rights so that the said Shelby should have liberty to take rights for the said land either in Virginia or North Carolina and gett Patents therefor, then said Shelby is to pay to John Cox Fifty pounds Virginia Cury., as well as thirty pounds, already paid in hand. In witness whereof I have hereunto sett my hand and seal this 4th day of February 1773.

Evan Shelby (L.S.) Signed sealed in the presence of John Fowler and John Shelby, and was proven by the Oath (p 163) of John Shelby a subscribing witness thereto and Ordered to be recorded.

JOHN ADAIR --------------Complts)
      agst   (In Equity
EDMUND WILLIAMS Ve ------Defts.)

                                For reasons appearing to the Court It is Ordered that this Cause be continued till the next term, and that Publication of the Testimony Pass.

JOHN AARONWINE -----------Complts.)
      agst   (In Equity
JOHN SHELEY --------------Deft.)

                             For reasons appearing to the Court, It is Ordered that this cause be continued till the next term, and that Commissions be awarded the parties to examine and take the depositions of their Witnesses, giving legal notice to the adverse party of the time and place of executing the same, which Commissions shall be executed within five months at the expiration of which time it is Ordered that publication of the Testimony do pass.

CHARLES HAYS -----------Complt.)
      agst   (In Equity
SAMUEL HARRIS -----------Deft.)

                             For reasons appearing to the Court It is Ordered that this suit be continued till the next term, and that Commissions be awarded the parties to examine and take the depositions of the witnesses in this Cause giving Legal notice of the time & place to the adverse party of the time & place of executing the same, which Commissions shall be executed within five months, at the expiration of which time it is Ordered that publication of the Testimony do pass.

(p 164)   ALEXANDER HAMILTON ----Complt)
                agst.   (Equity
            ROBERT PATTERSON ------Deft)

                             Ordered that Scire facias issue to receive the proceedings on this Cause.

JOHN WILLIAMS ESQRS. OF GRANVILLE COUNTY))
JAMES HOGG of ORANGE COUNTY in the State ((
of MARYLAND, Merchant and DAVID HART of (Complts (
CASWELL COUNTY GENT.   )) In Equity

```
                        agst.                                    )
The heirs and devisees of RICHARD HENDERSON                      (
late of GRANVILLE COUNTY decd, of NATHANIEL                      )
HART of --------COUNTY in VIRGINIA GENT. decd.                   (
of WILLIAM JOHNSTON, late of ORANGE COUNTY merchant              )
decd. of JOHN LUTTERALL of CHATHAM COUNTY Gentleman              (
dec'd. and LEONARD H. BULLOCK -------------------Defts           )
```

Some of the said heirs and devisees having failed to enter their appearance according to the Rules of this Court, and it appearing to the Satisfaction of the Court, that they reside without the limits of this Territory; on the motion of the said Complts by their attornies, It is ordered that unless the said heirs and devisees shall appear hereon the first day of the next term and answer the Bill of the Complts. that then it shall be taken for confessed and it is ordered that a copy of this Order be forthwith inserted in the Kentuckey Gazette, and the Newspaper regular published in Hagerstown for three weeks successively and at the front door of the Court house in the town of Jonesborough.

```
JOHN SHELBY ------------Complt)
        agst                  ( Instituted by Consent
WILLIAM BLEVINS --------Deft  )
```

For reasons appear- (p 165) ing to the Court It is Ordered that this Cause be continued till the next term.

```
GEORGE MARTIN -----------Complt. )
        agst.                    ( Equity
ANDREW ENGLISH --------Deft.     )
```

For reasons appearing to the Court, It is ordered that this suit be continued till the next term, and that Commissions be awarded the parties to examine and take the depositions of the witnesses in this Cause giving legal notice to the adverse party of the time and place of executing the same, which Commissions shall be executed within five months at the expiration of which time publication of the Testimony shall pass.

```
WILLIAM NELSON --------Complt.)
        agst                  ( Equity
JOHN HANNAH -----------Deft.  )
```

For reasons appearing to the Court, It is ordered that this suit be continued till the next term, and that Commissions be awarded the parties to examine and take the depositions of the Witnesses, giving legal notice of the time and place of executing the same.

```
HENRY MASSINGAL -------Complt.          )
        agst.                           ( Equity
DAVID HUGHES and JAMES STUART---Defts.)
```

For reasons appearing to the Court, It is Ordered that this cause be continued till the next term, and that Commissions be awarded to examine & take the depositions of the witnesses in this cause giving the adverse party Legal notice of the time and place of executing the same. And It is Ordered that Francis A. Ramsey a surveyor for the deft. and Jas. Greer a Surveyor (p 166) for the Complt. run out and Survey the lands in Dispute agreeably to the lines & bounds expressed in each partys title and make out three accurate plans of such Survey and return the same to the next term.

JOHN WADDEL ----------Complt)
  agst   (Equity
JAMES PATTERSON -----Deft)

       On the motion of the deft. by his atto. time
is giving him till tomorrow morning to put in his answer.

WILLIAM COX ----------Complt.)
  agst   (Equity
AUGUSTINE BRUMLEY ----Deft.)

       For reasons appearing to the Court It is Or-
dered that this Cause be Continued till the next term and that Commissions
be awarded the parties to examine and take the depositions of the witnesses
in this Cause giving the adverse party legal notice of the time & place of
executing the same.

MOSES HUMPHREYS ----------Complt.)
  agst   (Equity
MATTHEW TALBOT -----------Deft.)

       For reasons appearing to the Court It is
Ordered that this cause be Continued till the next term, and that Commissions be awarded to examine and take the depositions of the witnesses in this
suit giving the adverse party legal notice of the time and place of executing the same.

GEORGE MITCHEL --------Complt)
  agst   (Bill & Injunction
JOHN CARNEY -----------Deft.)

       The deft. having filed his answer to the bill
of the Complt. On the mo- (p 167) tion of the said deft. by his Attorney
It is Ordered that the Injunction Obtained by the Complt. agst. the deft. to
stay the proceedings at Law upon a Judgment Obtained by the said deft. against the Complt. at the last Superior Court for the district of Washington
in the Territory of the United States of America South of the River Ohio for
eighty pounds Current money and Costs be dissolved and the said Complt. pay
the Costs in this behalf expended.

WILLIAM ASHERT son and heir at Law)
to WILLIAM ASHERT decd ---------Complt (
    agst   ) Equity
JOHN COX Senr. JOHN COX Jur. (
and THOMAS AMIS ----------------Defts)

SAMUEL WILSON ------------------Complt.)
   agst   (Equity
ELISHA WALDEN ------------------Deft)

ROBERT KERR -------------------Complt)
   agst   (Equity
ALEXANDER MEEK ----------------Deft)

JOHN VANCE ---------------Complt)
  agst   (Equity
JOHN LAUGHLIN & ROBERT CRAIG)
Exrs. of the last Will & Testa- (
ment of JOHN LAUGHLIN decd.--Defts)

        For reasons appearing to the Court, It
is Ordered that the defts. in the foregoing suits have time till the next
term to put in their answers.

SAMUEL SMITH ------------Complt.)
  agst.   (Equity
PHILIP SAUNDERS & Exr.--Defts.)

       For reasons ap- (p 168) pearing to the
Court, It is Ordered that this Bill of the Complts be taken for Confessed
and that It be appointed to be heard exparte at the next term.

JAMES BRYANT -----------Complt)
  agst.   (Equity
JAMES HOUSTON the heirs of)
JOSEPH BULLARD decd and (
ALEXANDER OUTLAW -------Defts)

       The Demurrers of the said defts to the Bill
of the Complt being heard upon the arguments of the Council on both sides, It
seems to the Court here that the matters of fact alledged by the Complt
as they are set forth by himself are insufficient for him to proceed upon
or to oblige the said defts. to make answer unto. Therefore it is considered by the Court that the said defts. shall not be compelled to make any
other answer to the said Bill of Complt. and that the said defts recover
their Costs by them in this behalf expended.

DAVID BOOTHE ---------Complt)
  agst.   (Equity
BENJAMIN FORD & GANETT FITZGERALD-Defts)

       The Demurrer of the Defts. to the
Bill of the Complt. being heard upon the argument of the Counsel on both
sides and because the Court will advise thereupon, It is continued till
next Term.

JOHN WADDEL -------------Complt)
  agst.   (Equity
ROBERT PATTERSON --------Deft)

       The deft. having filed his answer on the
motion of the parties by their attornies It is Ordered that Commissions be
awarded them to examine and take the depositions of their Witnesses in this
suit.

(p 169) An Instrument of Writing from Peter Turney to Robert Sevier was
exhibited in Court which is in the words following:
"Know all men by these presents that I Peter Turney of Fincastle County
have bargained and sold unto Robert Sevier of the said place one certain
place and Improvement of Land lying between the Lands of Roger Topp, John

Shelby & John Beler the said Piece of Land I the said Turney purchased from John Beler now I the said Peter Turney do assign over & now deliver up all my right Title Claim and Command of the said Land and improvement unto the said Robert Sevier as it being for value Received of him witness my hand & seal this Ninth day of February 1774 Peter Turney (L.S.) Witness Present John Sevier, Robert Stuart, with an assignment thereon which is in the following words,

I assign over unto Mr John Shelby all my right Title claim and demand of the within Bill of Sale as witness my hand this ninth day of February 1774 Robert Sevier (L. S.) Witness present John Sevier and Robert Stuart and proven by the oath of the said John Sevier a subscribing witness thereto and Ordered to be recorded.

SIMON KIRKENDOLL----------Complt.)
      agst.   (Bill & Injunction
ROBERT MCAFEE ----------deft.)

                  Publication having been made in the Knoxville Gazette pursuant to the Order of the Court made at the last term and it appearing from the Testimony of Joseph Hadin & Charles Robinson Esqrs., that the full amount of the Judgment to which the Injunction in this cause was Obtained was paid to the said deft. on consideration whereof It is Decreed and Ordered that the Injunction aforesaid be made perpetual, and that the Complt. be enjoined from recovering the Judgment at Law mentioned in this Bill of Complt. and that the Complt. pay the (p 170) costs in this behalf expended and have execution agst. the sd., deft. for the same.

DAVID MCPETERS & CHARLES MCDOWELL -Complts)
      ags t   (Equity.
JOHN HERRITAGE, MARTIN CASWELL and)
ALEXANDER OUTLAW ----------------------Deft.)

                  On the motion of the defts by their Counsel It is Ordered that a commission be awarded to take the affidavit of John Herritage to his answer to the Bill of the Complts directed to the Hon^{oble} John Sitzreaves and it is further Ordered that the Bill be referred to the Clerk & Master and that he report whether the name of the deft. Martin Caswell be erased together with the necessary alterations consequent on such erasure, or remain as it now stands in the sd. Bill

SAMUEL WILSON ----------Plt.   ) Upon a Rule to shew a Cause why he should
      agst   (not be fined the sum of fifty pounds current
THOMAS BERRY ----------deft.) money for failing to deliver a copy of a Bill
                          in Equity agst. Elisha Walden when he served
him with a Subpoena.

                  For reasons appearing to the Court It is Ordered that the Judgment entered agst. the said deft. at the last term Nisi be remitted and that the plt. pay the Costs of this motion.
                Adjourned till Court in Course.

(p 171)
                At a Court of Equity begun and held in the town of Jonesborough on the fifteenth day of August one thousand Seven hundred and ninety two for the District of Washington, in the territory of the United States South of the River Ohio.

Present the Honorable
                    David Campbell) Judges
                    Joseph Anderson)

Archibald Roan produced a Commission in the words following (Viz) William
Blount Governor in and over the Territory of the United States of America
South of the River Ohio, To all who shall see these presents Greeting -
Know ye that I do appoint Archibald Roan of the County of Greene Clerk and
Master in Equity for the District of Washington and do authorize and em-
power him to execute and fulfil the duties of that Office according to law
and to have and to hold the said Office of Clerk and Master in Equity during his good behaviour or the existence of the temporary government of the
said territory with all the powers priviledges and Emoluments thereto of
right appertaining.
Given under my hand and Seal in the said Territory this Seventh day of
March One thousand seven hundred and ninety two (Signed) William Blount
(L.S.) By the Governor, Danl. Smith with a Certificate thereon that he
had taken an Oath to Support the Constitution of the United States and
the Oath of Office.

ArchibaldRoan entered into and acknowledged his Bond to the Judges together with Francis A. Ramsey, William Cooke and Landon Carter his securities
in the sum of two Thousand pounds; for the Safe keeping of the Records and
faithful performance of the duties of Clerk and Master in Equity.

(p 172)   CHARLES HAYS ------Complt)
                      vs   (Bill and Injunction
                 SAMUEL HARRIS -----Deft.   )

                                      By Consent of the parties and t
their Counsel on motion of the Counsel for the Complainant, It is Ordered
that the Publication of testimony on the behalf of the Complainant be prolonged till Wednesday evening the 21st Instant.

Friday the 23rd August 1792

WILLIAM BLEVINS and OTHERS - Complainant)
                      vs   (In Equity
JOHN SHELBY ------------------Defendant   )
                                      August 23rd, 24th, and 25th the
above Cause came onto be heard before the Honble David Campbell and Joseph
Anderson Esqr. Judges of said Court in the presence of Counsel learned in
the Law on both sides, the plaintiff's Bill and Defendants answere were
read the facts ascertained by verdicts found on the several issues directed were duly considered and the several paragraphs of Law and argument
offered by Counsel on both sides in Support of the Claims set forth in the
bill and answer were heard, and on debate investigation and hearing of the
matter, it appearing to the Court here that the plaintiff's have not Supported either an equitable or legal claim to the premises in dispute Claimed in the said Bill and the Defendant having Supported his equitable and
legal Claim set forth in his answer. It is thereupon considered by the
Court here and their Honours do order adjudge and decree that the Complainants Bill be dismissed and that the defendant John Shelby do recover against

the said Complainants his Costs etc.

DAVID MCPETERS and CHARLES MCDOWELL ---Complts)
                    vs   (Original Bill
ALEXANDER OUTLAW and JOHN HERRITAGE---Defts)

For reasons appearing to the
Court it is ordered that this suit be con- (p 173) tinued till next term
and that Commissions be awarded the Plaintiff and Defendants to take the
Depositions of their witnesses giving the adverse party legal notice of the
time and place of executing the same, which Commission shall be executed
within 5 months at the Expiration of which time publication of Testimony
shall pass.

WILLIAM BLEVINS --------Complt)
                    vs   (Bill and Injunction
JOHN BROWN -----------------Defendt.)

August 23rd, 24th & 25th the above Cause
Came on to be heard before the Honourable David Campbell and Joseph Anderson Esquires, Judges of said Court in presence of Counsel learned in the
Law on both sides, The Plaintiffs Bill and the defendants answer were read,
the facts ascertained by verdict found &c, were duly considered and the
several paragraphs of Law and arguments offered by Counsel on both sides in
Support of the Claims set forth in the bill and answer were heard; and on
debate investigation and hearing of the matter it appearing to the Court
here that the Plaintiff hath not Supported either an equitable or legal
Claim to the Premises in dispute Claimed in the said Bill and the defendant
having Supported his equitable and Legal Claim set forth in his answer It
is thereupon considered by the Court here and their Honours do order adjudge
and Decree that the Complainants Injunction here tofore obtained against
the Judgment of the said John Brown at Law be dissolved and that the Complainants bill be dismissed and that the said Defendant Recover against the
said Complainant his Costs.

JOHN ADAIR --------)
              vs   (Bill and Injunction
EDMOND WILLIAMS----)

This cause came on to be heard this day and on hearing
the Bill (p 174) and answer and proofs taken in the cause read, and hearing what was alledged by the Counsel on both sides and because the Court
will advise thereon, it is Continued till next term.

JNO. AARONWINE ---------Complt.)
                    vs   (Bill and Injunction
JOHN SHELBY -----------Defendt.)

For reasons appearing to the Court it is
ordered that this Cause be continued till next term and that publication be
prolonged for 5 months.

CHARLES HAYS - Complt.)
              vs   (Bill & Injunction
SAMUEL HARRIS -Deft.)

For reasons appearing to the Court It is ordered that

this Cause be continued till next term and that publication of testimony be prolonged and that a Commission be awarded the Complainant to take the Deposition of <u>Bates</u> and Commission to Defendant to take the deposition of William Sharpe and Ezekiel Smith

HENDERSON and COMPANY)
        vs   (Original Bill
HENDERSON and COMPANY)

        Some of the Heirs and Devisees having failed to enter their appearance according to the Rules of this Court and it appearing to the Satisfaction of the Court that they reside without the limits of this territory on the motion of said Complainants by their Attornies it is ordered that unless the said Heirs and Devisees shall appear on the first day of the next term and answer the Bill of the Complainants that then it shall be taken for confessed and that a Copy of this order be forthwith inserted in the Kentuckey Gazette and the newspaper regularly published in Hagerstown.

(p -175)   JOHN SHELBY ------------Complts   ) Instituted by consent
               vs   (to perpetuate Testimony.
    WILLIAM BLEVINS and OTHERS-Defendants)

                                 For reasons appearing to the Court it is Ordered that this Cause be dismissed at mutual Costs.

<u>DENSON</u> the Demise of JOHN SHELBY)
           vs   (Ejectment instituted by consent
WILLIAM BLEVINS and OTHERS   )

                          For reasons appearing to the Court it is Ordered that this Cause be continued till next term.

GEORGE MARTIN ------------Complt.)
          vs   (Bill and Injunction
ANDREW ENGLISH ---------Deft.)

                        For reasons appearing to the Court this Cause is ordered to be continued till next term and that Commissions be awarded to the parties to take depositions of their witnesses and that publication of Testimony pass at the Expiration of five months.

WILLIAM NELSON --------Complt)
          vs   (
JOHN HANNAH ------------Deft) For reasons appearing to the Court it is
                        ordered that this Cause be continued till next term and that Commissions be awarded the parties to take the depositions of their Witnesses, which Commissions shall be executed in five months at the expiration of which it is ordered that publication of Testimony do pass

WILLIAM BLEVINS ----------Complainant)
          vs   (
JOHN SHELBY --------------Defendant) Bill and Injunction

                              August 23rd, 24th and (p 176) 25th

this cause came on to be heard before the Honble David Campbell and Joseph Anderson Esqrs. Judges of said Court in the presence of Counsel learned in the law on both sides, the plaintiffs Bill and the defendants answer were read, the facts ascertained by verdicts found on the several issues directed were duely considered and the Several paragraphs of law and arguments offered by counsel on both sides in support of the Claims set forth in the Bill and answer were heard and on debate investigation and hearing of the matter it appearing to the Court here, that the Plaintiff hath not Supported either an equitable or legal title or claim to the premises in dispute claimed in the said Bill and the Defendant having supported his equitable and legal Claim and title set forth in his answer It is considered by the Court here and their Honours do order adjudge and decree that the Complainants Injunction heretofore obtained against the Judgment of the said John Shelby at law be dissolved and that the Complainants said Bill be dismissed and that the said John Shelby defendant do recover against the said Complainant his costs.

ALEXANDER HAMILTON --------Complainant)
         vs   (
JAMES PATTERSON -----------Defendant)

                    Ordered that a Scire facias issue to the Executors or administrator of the Defendant to revive the proceedings in this cause

HENRY MASSINGALE------------------------Complt.)
         vs   (Original Bill
DAVID HUGHES and JAMES STUART -------Deft.)

                    By Consent of the parties it is ordered that this cause be dismissed and that the Defendant, David Hughes pay his own Costs and James Stuart recover his Costs.

(p 177)   JOHN WADDELL -----------Complainant)
                vs   (Bill & Injunction
           ROBERT PATTERSON -------Defendant)

                    For reasons appearing to the Court it is ordered that this cause be continued till next term and that Commissions issue to the parties to take the Depositions of their Witnesses.

WILLIAM COX ------------------Complainant)
         vs   (Bill & Injunction
AUGUSTINE BRUMLEY ------------ Defendant)

                    Ordered that this cause be continued till next term and that Commissions be awarded to the parties to take the Depositions of their witnesses, which shall be executed within five months at the expiration of which time Publication of the testimony shall pass.

PETER MCCALL -----------Complainant)
         vs   (Original Bill
JOHN EGAN -------------Defendant)

                    For reasons appearing to the Court it is ordered that the Rule of Reference heretofore made in this Cause be set aside and that the Defendant put in his answer to the Bill.

MOSSES HUMPHREYS ----------Complainant)
        vs   (Bill and Injunction
MATTHEW TALBOT -------------Defendant)

On motion of the Defendant by his Attorney (after reading the Complainants Bill and the answer of the Defendant and hearing the arguments of Counsel on both sides) it is ordered by the Court that the Complainants injunction heretofore obtained against Judgment at Law of the Said Defendant be dissolved and that thesaid Complainant pay the Costs in this behalf expended

By consent of the said Complainant it is fur- (p 178) ther Ordered that his Bill of Complaint be dismissed and that the Defendant Matthew Talbot do recover against the said Complainant his Costs

GEORGE MITCHELL -----Complt)
        vs   (In Equity
JOHN CARNEY -------Defendant)

By consent of the Plaintiffs Attorney it is ordered that this Suit be Dismissed.

WILLIAM ASHERT ----------------------Complt.)
        vs   (Original Bill
JOHN COX Senr. JOHN COX Jur and (
THOMAS AMIS ----------------------Defts.)

The defendants having filed their several answers to the Complainants bill it is ordered that this cause be continued till next term and that Commissions be awarded to the parties to take the depositions of their witnesses.

SAMUEL WILSON ------Complainant)
        vs   (Bill of Injunction
ELISHA WALDEN ------Defendant)

The Defendant having filed his answer to the Complainants bill, It is ordered that this Cause be continued till next term and that Commissions be awarded the parties to take the depositions of their Witnesses.

ROBERT KERR -----------Complt.)
        vs   (Bill and Injunction
ALEXANDER MEEK --------Deft.)

The Defendant having filed his answer to the Complainants bill It is ordered that this Cause be continued till next term and that Commissions issue to the parties to take the Depositions of their witnesses.

(p 179)   JOHN VANCE --------Complainant   )
                vs   (Original Bill
            JOHN LAUGHLIN &   )   )
            ROBERT CRAIG EXTS. of the ((
            Last will and Testament of)Defendants)
            JOHN LAUGHLIN DECEASED   )   (

AUSTIN SHOAT ----------Complt.)
        vs   (Bill and Injunction
EPHRAIM DUNLAP --------Deft.)

JOHN SHIRLEY ----------Compt)
        vs   (In Equity
JOHN GILLILAND --------Deft.)

For reasons appearing to the Court it is Ordered that the Defendants in the foregoing Suits have time till the next term to plead Answer or Demur.

SAMUEL SMITH ------------Complt.)
        vs   (
PHILIP SAUNDERS)   (In Equity
  and   (Defendants (
MARY SAUNDERS)   )

On Motion of the Attorney for the Complainant and for reasons appearing to the Court it is Ordered that the Rule that the Complainants be taken pro Confesso entered at last term be set aside at the Complaints Costs and a Sub poena Issue to the Defendants to put in their answer to the Complaints Bill

JOHN TYE -------------Complts)
       vs   (Bill and Injunction
DAVID REESE ----------Deft)

On Motion of the Complainants Attorney it is ordered that a Subpoena issue to Hawkins County for the Defendant to put in his answer to theComplainants bill.

(p 180)   DAVID BOOTHE -----------Complt.)
                  vs   (
             BENJAMIN FORD   )   ) In Equity
                &   (------Deft. (
             GARRETT FITZGERALD)   )

The Demurrer of the Defendants to the bill of the Complainant being read and on argument of the Counsel on both sides It is ordered that the Demurrer of the Defendant be over ruled and that they put in their answer to the Complainants Bill.

Court adjourned till Court in Course.

(p 181) At a Court of Equity begun and held at the Court house in Jonesborough for the District of Washington in the Territory of the United States of America South of the River Ohio on the fifteenth day February one thousand Seven hundred and Ninety three.

Present the Honourable
         David Campbell)
            and   (Judges
         Joseph Anderson)

DAVID McPETERS and CHARLES McDOWELL)
      vs   (
ALEXANDER OUTLAW, JOHN HERRITAGE)

            By the consent of the parties and
their Attornies it is ordered that this Cause be dismissed and that the
Costs be taxed according to a written agreement filed.

JOHN AARONWINE ---------Complainant)
      vs   (Bill and Injunction
JOHN SHELBY ------------Defendant)

            By consent of both parties by their
Attornies it is ordered that this cause be continued till next term.

JOHN ADAIR ------------------Compt)
      vs   (Bill and Injunction
EDMOND WILLIAMS ------------ Deft.)

            This day came the parties by their At-
tornies and thereupon Came also a Jury (towit) George Doherty, Samuel
Wilson, Nicholas Perkins Thomas Henderson, Thomas Hutchings, John Patterson
John Shelby, James White, Asahel Rawlings, George McNutt, George Vincent
and David Caswell who being duly sworn well and truly to enquire what damages Edmond Williams hath Sustained by reason of John Adair failing to send
him certain prooffs according to Contract upon their Oaths do say (p 182)
that they assess the damages sustained by Edmond Williams by reason of the
failure of John Adair to one hundred and thirty pounds fifteen shillings

Whereupon and on hearing the Bill and answer read and what could be alledged by the counsel on both sides and on debate and Investigation of the matter it is considered by the Court and their Honours do order adjudge and
Decree that the Injunction for the Sum of thirty four pounds Seventeen
Shillings of the Judgment obtained by the said Edmond Williams at Law be
made perpetual and that the injunction for the residue of the said Judgment
that is to say for the Sum of one hundred and thirty four pounds fifteen
shillings be dissolved and that the said Edmond Williams have the Benefit
of his Judgment at Law for the said Sum of one hundred and thirty four
pounds fifteen shillings
    And the Court do further order and decree that the Complainant John
Adair do recover against the said Edmond Williams his costs in this behalf
expended.
    Ordered that the foregoing decree be signed and enrolled.

CHARLES HAYS ------------Compt.)
      vs   (Bill and Injunction
SAMUEL HARRIS --------Defendt.)

            Ordered by the Court with the assent of
the parties that the following Issues of fact be tried by a Jury in this
Cause viz,

1st Whether Aaron Burlison, Jesse Bounds, Stephen Harris and Thomas Bates
or some of them from whom Charles Hays the Complainant derives his title
had made any lawful Improvement on the premises in dispute before opening

the Land office in the year 1778. (p 183) 2nd Whether Thomas Bates entered a claim for the premises in dispute, before the first day of January
in the year 1779.

Whereupon came the parties by their Attornies and also Came a Jury
Viz.

1 George Dougherty, 5 George McNutt, 9 Thomas Gillaspie
2 Thomas Hutchings, 6 George Vincient, 10 Adam Meek
3 John Patterson, 7 David Caldwell 11. Thomas Rodgers &
4 John Nelson, 8 Ananias McCoy 12. Archibald Blackburn, who being duly sworn
and impannelled to try the first Issue before mentioned on their Oaths do say
that Aaron Burleson, Jesse Bounds, Stephen Harris Thomas Bates or some of
them from whom Charles Hays the Complainant derives his title made a Lawful
improvement on the premises in dispute before opening the Land office in the
year 1778.

The Defendant Samuel Harris in open Court admits that Thomas Bates
entered a Claim for the premises in dispute before the first day of January
in the year 1779.

This cause came on to be heard and the Bill and answer being read and the
Arguments of Counsel on both sides heard and because the Court will advise
thereon it is ordered to be Continued till next term.

GEORGE MARTIN ------Complt)
            vs   (Bill and Injunction
ANDREW ENGLISH ------Deft)

WILLIAM COX ----------Complt)
            vs   (Bill and Injunction
AUGUSTINE BROWLEY -----Deft)
                            By consent of the parties and their Attornies
it is ordered that the above Cause be Continued till next term.

(p 184)

WILLIAM NELSON ------Complt)
            vs   (Bill and Injunction
JOHN HANNAH ----------Deft)
                            This day Came William Cocke Attorney for the
Complainant and Dismissed the Bill of the said William Nelson.

HENDERSON and COMPANY)
            vs   (Original Bill
HENDERSON and COMPANY)
                    Some of the Heirs and Devisees having failed to enter
their appearance according to the Rules of this Court and it appearing to the
Satisfaction of this Court that they reside without the limits of this Territory: on motion of the said Complainants by their Attorney it is ordered that
unless the said Heirs and Devisees shall appear here on the first day of the
next term and answer the Bill of the Complainants that then it shall be taken
pro. Confesso: and that a Copy of this order be forthwith published for two
weeks Successively in some Gazette regularly published in the State of Mary-

land and in the State of Kentucky

DEW on the Demise of JOHN SHELBY)
        vs   (Ejectment Instituted by consent.
WILLIAM BLEVENS and OTHERS)

                For reasons appearing to the Court is is ordered that a Writ of Possession issue to the Sheriff of Sullivan County to put John Shelby in possession of the premises in the Declaration of Ejectment Specified.

ALEXANDER HAMILTON ------Complt)
        vs   (Original Bill
JAMES PATTERSON ----------Deft)

                John Scott Sheriff of Sullivan County made return that he had made known the Scire facias to the representatives of (p 185) James Patterson Deceased
It is thereupon ordered by the Court that this suit be revived - and on motion of the Attorney for the Defendant it is ordered that a Scire facias issue to the Plaintiff to show cause why he should not give better Security for the prosecution of his Bill of Complaint.

JOHN WADDELL -----------Complt)
        vs   (Bill and Injunction
ROBERT PATTERSON---------Deft)

WILLIAM ASHERT -----------Complt)
        vs   (
JOHN COX Senior   )   ) Original Bill
JOHN COX Junr. and(Defts. (
THOMAS AMIS   )   )

ROBERT KERR ---------Complt.)
        vs   (Bill and Injunction
ALEXANDER MEEK ------Deft.)

                For reasons appearing to the Court it is Ordered that these Causes be continued till next term and that commissions issue to the parties to take the depositions of their witnesses

PETER MCCALL -------Compt)
        vs   (Original Bill
JOHN EGAN --------Deft.)

                This Cause is ordered to be continued till next term for the Defendant to put in his answer to the Complainants Bill.

SAMUEL WILSON --------Complts)
        vs   (
ELISHA WALDEN --------Deft)

                This cause is ordered to be continued till next term and that Commissions issue to the parties to take the Depositions of their Witnesses (p 186) which Commissions shall be executed within six months at the expiration of which time publication of the testimony shall pass.

JOHN VANCE ------------Complt.)
      VS   (Original Bill
JOHN LAUGHLIN and)
ROBERT CRAIG   )   Defts)

          The parties having submitted to arbitration all the matters and things respecting this cause and the arbitration having returned their award to this Court it is ordered that the same be filed and Confirmed.

SAMUEL SMITH -------Compt.)
     VS   (
PHILIP SAUNDERS and) Defts (Original Bill
MARY his wife   (   )

         The Demurrer of the Defendant to the Bill of the Complainant being heard and on argument of the Councel on both sides it is considered by the court that the said Defendants shall not be compelled to make any other answer to the said Bill and that the said Defendant recover their Costs by them in this behalf expended.

WILLIAM COCKE --------Compt)
     VS   (Original Bill
RICHARD HENDERSON)   (
and COMPANY   (Defts)

         It is ordered that this Cause be continued till next term.

JOHN TYE ------------Compt)
     VS   (Bill and Injunction
DAVID REESE --------Deft)

         The Defendant David Reese having failed to enter his appearance according to the Rules of this Court and it appearing to the Satisfaction of the Court that he is not an inhabitant of this (p 187) Territory it is ordered that the said David Reese do appear at our next Superior Court of Equity to be held for the district of Washington at Jonesborough on the third Monday of September next and answer the Bill of Complainant, otherwise it will be taken pro confesso and the matter thereof decreed accordingly and that a Copy of this order be inserted in the Knoxville Gazette

DAVID BOOTHE ----------Comp)
     VS   (Bill
BENJAMIN FORD and) Defts)
GARRETT FITZGERALD)   )

         The Defendants having filed their answers to the Bill of the Complainant. It is ordered that commission issue to the parties to take the Depositions of their Witnesses.

AUSTIN SHOAT----------Complt.)
     VS   (Injunction
EPHRAIM DUNLAP ------Deft.)

         It is ordered with consent of the parties by

their Attornies that time of three months be given to the Defendant to put in his answer and that Commission issue to the parties to examine their Witnesses

JOHN SHIRLEY ------------Compt.)
           vs   (Bill
JOHN GILLILAND --------Deft.)

THOMAS HUTCHINGS -----Compt)
        vs   (Injunction
HENRY CONWAY --------Defts)

                   For reasons appearing to the Court it is ordered that the defendants in these Causes have time till next term to plead answer or Demur.

(p 188)   WILLIAM GARDINER ---Compt   )
                vs   (
           MANY LOONEY and the   ) Defts) Bill
           Heirs of BENJAMIN LOONEY DECD(   )

                   Time is given the Defend ants till next term to put in their answer to the Complainants Bill and it is ordered by the Court that Walter Johnston be appointed Guardian for the orphans of Benjamin Looney Deceased to Defend this Suit on their behalf

Court adjourned till the third Monday of September next.

(p 189) At a Court of Equity begun and held for the District of Washington within the territory of the United States of America South of the River Ohio in the Court House of the County of Washington 25th day of September one thousand Seven Hundred and ninety Three.

Present The Honble.
        David Campbell)
            &   (Esqrs.
        Joseph Anderson)

Landon Carter Produced a Commission which is in the words following towit William Blount Governor in and over the Territory of the United States of America South of the River Ohio, To all who shall see these Presents Greetings, Know ye that I do appoint Landon Carter esq. Clerk and Master in Equity for the District of Washington to have and to hold the said Office of Clerk and Master in Equity for the District aforesaid with all Powers, Priviledges and Emoluments there to belonging during his Good behaviour or during the Existance of the temporary Government thereof. Given under my hand and Seal at Knoxville in the Territory aforesaid this thirtyeth day of March one Thousand Seven Hundred and ninety three Signed William Blount with a Certificate thereon that he had taken and Oath to Support the Constitution of the United States and the oath of Office.

JOHN AARONWINE   )
      vs   (Bill & Injunction
JOHN SHELBY   )

Ordered that the following Issue of Fact be tried in the above Cause whether the Right of Preocupation to the Four Hundred acres of Land now in dispute be vested in John Aaronwine by Purchase from those under whome he claims or in John Shelby by Purchase from those under (p190) whom he claims.

A Jury Impanneled and Sworn to wit, Joseph Brittain, James Sevier, Samuel Honley, Walter Johnston, John Meliken, John Blair, Thomas Vincient, Michael Rawlings, John Beard, John Wear of Washington Joel Gillenwaters and John Strain on their Oaths Say they find the Right of Preocupation to the Four Hundred acres of Land in dispute to be vested in the Plaintiff John Aaronwine by Purchase from those under whome he Claims.

JOHN AARONVIN -----Compt)
vs   (Bill & Injunction
JOHN SHELBY -------Deft.)

Wednesday the 25th of September 1793 the above Cause came on to be heard before the Honbl. Joseph Anderson Esqr. a Judge of the said Court in the Presents of Council Learned in the Law on both sides the Plaintiffs Bill and defendants answer being read and the Facts ascertained by verdicts found or Issues directed to be tried having been duly weighed and Considered the Several Paragraphs of Law and arguments of Council offered on both sides in Support of the Claims set forth in the Bill and answer was heard and on mature deliberation, thereupon It is considered by the Court here that the said John Aaronwine the Complainant hath Supported his Equitable Claim to the Premises in dispute as set forth in his Bill, and his Honour doth thereupon adjudge and Decree that the said Injunction to the Judgment at Law of him the said John Shelby be and the same is hereby made absolute and perpetual and his Honour doth further order adjudge and decree that the Said Grant of the said John Shelby whereupon he Recovered at Law for so much thereof as fell within the Lands of the Said John Aaronwines Land aforesaid be and the Same is hereby annuled and made void and of no Effect and that the Said John Aaronwines Recover his Costs Except his own Attorney's Fee and that the said John Shelby be liable to all (p 191) the Costs in the Court of Law in his Suit in Ejectment by Complainants Bill injoined.

CHARLES HAYS -------Compt.)
vs   (Bill & Injunction
SAMUEL HARRIS -----Deft.)

Wednesday the 25th of September 1793 the foregoing Cause came on to be heard before the Honble. Joseph Anderson Esqr. a Judge of said Court, in the presence of Counsel learned in the Law on both sides, the plaintiffs Bill and Defendants answer were Read and the facts ascertained by verdicts found on the Issues directed to be tried, having been duly weighed & considered the several Paragraphs of Law and Arguments of Counsel offered on both sides in Support of the Claims set forth in the Bill and answer were heard and on mature deliberation thereupon it is considered by the Court here, that the said Charles Hays Plt. hath supported his equitable Claim to the Premises in dispute as set forth in his Bill and his Honour doth thereupon adjudge and Decree that the Said Injunction to the Judgment at Law of him the said Samuel Harris be and the same is hereby made absolute and Perpetual and his Honour doth

further order adjudge and decree that the SaidGrant of him the said Samuel
Harris whereupon he Recovered at Law for so much thereof as falls within
the Lines of the Said Charles Hays's Land aforesaid be and the Same is hereby annuled and made Void, and of no Effect and that the Said Charles Hays
recover his costs in this Honble. Court and that the sd. Samuel Harris be
liable for the Costs at Law in his Suit by Ejectment by the Complainants
Bill injoined.

(p 192)   GEORGE MARTIN ---Compt)
                        vs   (Bill & Injunction
        ANDREW ENGLISH--Defendt)

                              This day came the Parties by their
attornies and thereupon came also a Jury to wit, Joseph Brittain John Wear
of Green, Andrew Greer, James Sevier, Walter Johnston, Thomas Vincent,
John Beard, John Wear of Washington, Joel Gillenwaters, John Meligen,Joseph
Hardin and Dillen Blevins who being sworn well and truely to inquire whether Andrew English by himself or agent did take actual and Peaceable Possession of the Lands now in dispute and Peaceably begin the first Improvement
and carry on the Same by Cuting Logs for a House bringing the same together
and Raising the said House before the said George Martin came to take Possession of the said Land; upon their oaths do say they find the Facts as
Stated in the above Issue in favour of the Defendant Andrew English.

    And the foregoing Jurors being Sworn well and truely to enquire wheth-
er George Martin by himself or others availed himself of Force or threats to
Prevent said Englishes Improvement from being completed as a Lawfull, Im-
provement such as is now Riquisate by act of assembly upon their Oaths do
Say they find in Favour of the defendant Andrew English and the aforesaid
Jurors being Sworn well and truely to inquire whether the Complainant George
Martin directed or by his agent consented to any act which Prevented Andrew
English or his agent from Compleating a Lawfull Improvement on the Lands in
dispute as is Required by the Laws of North Carolina upon their oaths say
that George Martin did not direct or by his agent Consent to any act which
prevented Andrew English or his agent from Compleating such lawfull Improvement on the Lands in dispute as is Required by the Laws of North Carolina
(p 193) For reasons appearing to the Court it is ordered that the foregoing
Cause be Continued untill next Term.

WILLIAM COX ------Compt)
        vs   (Bill & Injunction
AUGUSTINE BRUMLEY --Deft)

                         For reasons appearing to the Court it is ordered
that this cause be continued till the next Term and that Commissions Issue
to take depositions in this Cause on giving Legal notice of time and place
of executing the Same.

HENDERSON and COMPANY - Compt.)
        vs   (Original Bill
HENDERSON and COMPANY -Deft.)

                       For reasons appearing to the Court it is
order_ that this Cause be Continued till next Term and Rule of Publication
answered.

ALEXANDER HAMILTON ---Complt.)
     vs   (Original Bill
JAMES PATTERSON ----Deft.)

        Scire facis Returned not found by John McKay
Deputy Sheriff Sullivan County and on motion of the attorney for the defendant it is Ordered that Publication be made in the Knoxville Gazette
that the Complainant appear at next Term and Shew cause why he should not
give better Security for the Prosecution of his Bill of Complaint or else
his Suit will be dismissed.

JOHN WADDLE ---Complt.)
     vs   (Bill & Injunction
ROBERT PATTERSON -Deft.)

        It appearing to the Court that the Bail of the
Defendant is insufficient and on motion of the Attorney for the Complainant this Ordered that unless the Defendant appear on the first day of the
next Term and Give Better Security the Bill of Com- (p 194) plaint will
be taken Pro Confesso and that a Copy of this order be forth with inserted
in the Knoxville Gazette and that Commissions be awarded to the Complainant to take depositions of his Witnesses

PETER MCCALL ------Complt.)
     vs   (Original Bill
JOHN FEGAN --------Deft.)

        The defendant having filed his answer the first
day of the Term, it is Ordered that this Cause be continued untill next
Term and that Commissions be awarded the Parties to take the Depositions
of their witnesses.

WILLIAM ASHERT ------Compt)
     vs   (
JOHN COX Senr   )) Original Bill
JOHN COX Junr. and(Defts (
THOMAS AMIS))

        For Reasons appearing to the Court it is ordered that this cause be continued untill next Term and that Commissions
Issue to the Parties to take the depositions of their Witnesses directed
to Colo. Henderson of Hawkins County to take the Same.

SAMUEL WILLSON ------Complt.)
     vs   (Original Bill
ELISHA WALDEN ------Deft.)

        For Reasons appearing to the Court it is ordered that this Cause be continued untill next Term and by consent of the
Parties no exceptions is to be taken to depositions heretofore taken in this
Cause before James White and Thomas Amis Esqes. and that Commissions be awarded to both Parties to take the Depositions of their Witnesses.

(p 195) ROBERT KERR ----Complt.)
      vs   (Bill and Injunction
    ALEXANDER MEEK--Deft)

for Reasons appearing to the Court this Cause Continued &
Commissions awarded for both Parties.

JOHN VANCE ------------Complt)
              vs   (Original Bill
JOHN LAUGHLIN &)   (
ROBERT CRAIG) ------Defts)
                          Ordered that the Costs not Provided for by
the award filed be divided in Proportion to the Costs awarded.

WILLIAM COCKE ----------Compt.   )
              vs   (Original Bill
RICHARD HENDERSON & COMPANY-Defts)
                          For Reasons appearing to the Court this
Cause Continued untill next Term.

JOHN TIGH --------Compt.)
              vs   (Bill & Injunction
DAVID REESE--------Deft.)
                          For Reasons appearing to the Court it is Ordered
that time be given Defendant David Reese untill next Term to put in his answer.

DAVID BOOTH -------Compt)
              vs   (Original Bill
BENJAMIN FORD &   (
GARRETT GITZGERALD -Defts) For Reasons appearing to the Court it is ordered
                          that this Cause be Continued untill next term and
Rule for Publication at the end of Five months and Commissions awarded for
both Parties

(p 196) AUSTIN SHOAT -------Compt.)
              vs   (Bill and Injunction
         EPHRAIM DUNLAP -----Deft.)
                          Defendants answer filed the 13th of
Augt. 1793 & the Plaintiffs exceptions filed 25th Sept. 1793 on motion of
the Plaintiff by his attorney it is Ordered that the Defendant put in a more
full andPerfect answer within three months.

JOHN SHIRLEY --------Compt.)
              vs   (Original Bill
JOHN GILLALAND -------Deft.)
                          For Reasons appearing to the Court it is ordered
that this cause be continued untill next Term and the defendant allowed a
further time of Sixty Days to put in his answer.

THOMAS HUTCHINGS -------Compt.)
              vs   (Bill & Injunction
HENRY CONWAY -----------Deft.)
                          Answer filed
                          On Reading Bill and answer it

ordered that the Injunction be dissolved and the Bill dismissed.

WILLIAM GARDINER--------Compt.)
     vs   (Original Bill
MARY LOONEY & the Heirs of)Defts. (
BENJAMIN LOONEY Deceased))

           Ordered by the Court that the Bill of the
Complainant be taken Pro-confesso unless the answer of the defendant be filed
within one Hundred Days.

ALEXANDER MCFARLAND--Compt.)
    vs   (Bill & Injunction
ROBERT HOOD----------Deft.)

        For Reasons appearing to the Court it is Ordered
that Scire facias Issue to the Executors or administrators of the Defendant
Robert (p 197) Hood to Shew Cause why this Suit Should not Revive.

JOHN CARNEY ----------Compt)
   vs   (
EPHRAIM W. DUNLAP)) Original Bill
  & (Defts (
ANNE MOORE)   )

        For Reasons appearing to the Court it is ordered
that Ephraim Dunlap one of the defendants put in a more full and Perfect answer than the one filed by the next Term also that Publication be made in the
Knoxville Gazette that Anne Moore appear here at the next Term and put in her
answer to the Complainants Bill or else it will be taken for Confessed to her.

Court adjourned untill the third Monday in March next.

(p 198) At a Court of Equity begun and Held for the District of Washington
within the Territory of the United States of America South of the River Ohio
in the Court House of the County of Washington the third Monday in March 1794.

Present The Honbl David Campbell)
     and   (Esqrs
   Joseph Anderson)

GEORGE MARTIN ----Compt.)
    vs   (Bill & Injunction.
ANDREW INGLISH ---Defendt)

        On motion of the Defendants Attorney It is Or-
dered that a new Trial be granted in the last Issue tried in this Suit at
September Term 1793 -
      Whereupon there Came a Jury impaneled Tried & and Sworn (to wit)
Thomas Henderson, David Larkin, John Jones, Nathaniel Davis, Binone Perimon,
Robert Allison, David Russell, Alexd Greer, Leeroy Taylor, John Waddle and John
Beard, who upon their Oaths Say they find for the Complainant George Martin,
that he did not direct or by his agent consent to any thing that prevented
Andrew Inglish from making a Lawfull Improvement as is Reqd by the laws of
North Carolina on March 26th 1794 the foregoing cause came on to be heard

before the Honble David Campbell and Joseph Anderson Esqrs. Judges of Said
Court in Presents of Council Learned in the Law on both Sides the Plaintiffs
Bill and Defendants answer being Read and the facts ascertained by Verdicts
found on the Issues directes to be tryed. It is Ordered by the Court that
the Complainants Bill of Injunction be Dissolved.

(p 199)   WILLIAM COX -----Compt.)
                vs   (Bill & Injunction
              AUGUSTINE BRUMLEY-Deft.)
                        On motion of the Defendant by his
Attorney It is ordered that this Bill and Injunction of the Complainant be
Dissolved.

HENDERSON and COMPANY)
        vs   (Original Bill
HENDERSON and COMPANY)
                        For Reasons appearing to the Court, It is ordered
that this Cause be continued untill next Term and Rule for Publication be
Renewed in the Kentucky Gazette.

ALEXANDER HAMILTON ---Compt.)
        vs   (Original Bill
JAMES PATTERSON ------Deft)

JOHN WADDLE --------Compt.)
        vs   (Bill and Injunction
ROBERT PATTERSON ----Deft.)
                        For Reasons appearing to the Court It is Or-
dered that the foregoing Causes be Continued untill next Term and Rule of
Publication be inlarged untill next Term

PETER MCCALL------Compt)
        vs   (Original Bill
JOHN JUGAN------Defendt.)
                        On motion of the Defendant by his Attorney after
Reading the Complaints Bill and Defendants Answer It is ordered that the
Bill of the Complainant be Dismissed.

WILLIAM ASHERST------Compt)
        vs   (Original Bill
JOHN COX Senr.   )   )
JOHN COX Junr and (Defts (
THOMAS AMIS   )   )
(p200) This Cause dismissed by consent of Plaintiff and Defendants they be
ing Present Plaintiff Paying his own Attorneys Fee and the Defendants to be
taxed with the Residue of the Cost, and this agreement to stand as a final
Settlement between the Parties to the Present date __

SAMUEL WILLSON ----- Compt.)
  vs ((Bill & Injunction
ELISHAE WALDON)---- Deft)

    For Reasons appearing to the Court it is or-
dered that this Cause be continued untill next term and Rule for Commissions for Plaintiff

WILLIAM COOKE ---------Compt)
  vs (Original Bill
RICHARD HENDERSON &
COMPANY ------------Deft)

    For Reasons appearing to the Court it is Order-
ed that this Cause be continued untill the next Term.

JOHN TIGH ---------Compt)
  vs (Bill & Injunction
DAVID REES --------Deft)

    For Reasons appearing to the Court it is Ordered
that this Cause be Continued untill the next term and Publication inlarged
in the Knoxville Gazette

DAVID BOOTH -------Compt
  vs
BENJAMIN FORD and) Defts
GARRET FITZGERALD)

    The foregoing Cause came on to be heard before the Hon
ourable David Campbell and Joseph Anderson Esqrs., Judged of the Court aforesaid in presents of Council Learned in the Law on both Sides the Complainants Bill and the Defendants answer being Red (p 201) It is Ordered
by the Court that the Complainants Bill be dismissed.

AUSTON SHOAT -----Compt)
  vs (Original Bill
JOHN GILLALAND ---Deft)

    The foregoing Cause Came on to be heard before
the Court in presents of Council Learned in the Law on both Sides the Complainants Bill and Defendants answer being Red, It is ordered that Complainants Bill be Dismissed.

WILLIAM GARDNER-------Compt)
  vs   (Original Bill
MARY LOONEY and the Heirs) (
of BENJAMIN LOONEY Deceased)Defend)

    For Reasons appearing to the Court It
is ordered that this Cause be Continued untill next Term and that Mary
Looney answer with Four months also Rule for Commissions for Complainant
and defendant.

ALEXANDER MCFARLAN---Compt)
  vs (Bill & Injunction
ROBERT HOOD ---------Deft)

For Reasons appearing to the Court It is Ordered that this Cause be continued untill next Term and that James Richardson one of the defendants put in an answer within Three months also Comissions awarded for Complainant and defendant.

```
JOHN CARNEY ------------------Compt.)
            vs                      (
EPHRAIM DUNLAP and) Defendt         ( Bill & Injuncsion
ANNE MOORE         (                )
```

For Reasons appearing to the Court it is Ordered that this be continued untill next term and Rule of Publication inlarged untill the next Term.

```
(p 202)   ROBERT KEER ------Compt)
              vs                 ( Bill & Injunction
          ALEXANDER WEEK----Deft.)
```

For Reasons appearing to the Court it is Ordered that this Cause be Continued untill the next term and Comissions awarded for Complainent and defendant.

```
WILLIAM BLEVINS ------Compt )
            vs              ( Bill & Injunction
JOHN SHELBY------Defendant  )
```

On Petition it is ordered that a new Trial be Granted in this cause and it ordered by the Court that   Issue to the Defendant.

```
JOSEPH RANNALS --------Compt      )
            vs                    (
RUTH TOOL administratrix )        ) Original Bill
ARCHIBALD ROAN and        ( Defts(
JOHN HACKET administrators(       (
of JOHN TOOL Deceased    )        )
```

For Reasons appearing to the Court it is ordered that this Cause be Continued untill next term and on motion it is further ordered that Archibald Roan be appointed Guardian to this Suit in behalf of the Orphans ----

```
JOHN GILLILAND --------Compt.)
            vs               ( Bill & Injunction
JOHN SHIRLEY----------Deft.)
```

On motion it is ordered by the Court that this Suit be continued untill the next term and Comissions to Issue for Complainant and Defendant by Consent ----

```
JOHN HANNAH------------------------Compt )
            vs                           ( Fi Fa
CHARLES ROBINSON &          )            (
JORDAN ROACH SECURITIES ( Defendants     )
for WILLIAM NELSON          )            ) Sci Fa
```

Executed on (p 203) Charles Robinson and Service
acknowledged, also Executed on Jordan Roach in Presence of Thomas Berry
& James Reed _____

      Geo. Gillespie per Shff.

It is ordered by the Court that Judgment be awarded against the Bail in
the Suit.

Court adjourned untill the third Monday in September next ____

(p 204) At a Court of Equity begun and held for the District of Washington at the Court House in Jonesborough on Tuesday the 16th of September
1794.

Present the Honourable,

    David Campbell) Esqr
    John McNairy & (Judges of
    John Anderson) Said Court.

John Carter Produced a Commission Vesting him with the appointment of
Clerk and Master in Equity for the District of Washington, Signed William
Blount to which Commission he qualified as the Law directs.

WILLIAM BLEVINS ------------Compt)
    vs   (Bill & Injunction
JOHN SHELBY ------------Defend)

       On Friday the 26th of September this
Cause Came on to be heard before the Honourable Court and Counsil learned
in the Law on both Sides the Plaintiffs Bill and defendants answer were
red and duely considered, and the Several paragraphs of Law and arguments
offered by Counsil on both sides in Support of the Claims set for in the
Bill answer were heard, and on debate Investigation and hearing of the
matter, It is ordered by the Court here that the Petition of the Complainant for a Rehearing be set aside and that the Claim of the Defendant be
confirmed. From which order the Complainant prayed an appeal to the Superior Federal Court of the United States to be held in the city of Phila-
delphia which was granted for reasons filed as follows (to wit).
1st. It appears from the Depositions that the defendant came to the Land in
dispute and probably some other persons about the year 1773 soon after he
had made a purchase under a Grant from the State of Virginia and found the
plaintiff Settled on the Said Land which was the first notice the plaintiff
Received of the defendants Claim.
(p 205) 2nd It appears from the pleadings and Exhibits that the Said disput-
ed Land was Situated within the Limits of North Carolina after the extention
of the Boundary Line between that State and Virginia

3rd That the plaintiff in Order to Secure his Rights acquired by Occupancy
and under the Idea that the Land would fall within the State of North Carolina
in the months of Jany and October 1779 paid the Consideration to the State of
North Carolina and made two Entries according to law and afterwards obtained
a Grant thereupon.

4th That the assembly of North Carolina in the year 1782 passed a law declaring the Grant under which the Defendant claimed valid.

5th The Counsel for the Plaintiff Supposing that his first occupancy agreeable to the Laws of nature gave him an Equitable title to the land which being afterwards confirmed by his Enteries and the Grant obtained from North Carolina for the same and Supposing that the act of 1782 is a violation of the laws of Contracts of nature the unalienable rights of man and the Constitution of the State In as much as the Legislature in passing the act aforesaid assumed a right which was not nor Could have been conceded by the Said Constitution to wit,
The disposition of private property and the Effectual Prosecution of the aforesaid appeal the Complainant William Blevins gave Dillen Blevins and John Carter Securities who were bound in Eight Hundred Dollars.

WILLIAM BLEVINS ------Compt)
     vs   (
JOHN BROWN ------------Deft.)

On Rehearing the two last suits it is ordered by the Court here that the Petition for Rehearing be set aside and the claim of the Defendants be confirmed and appeal Prayed and (p 206) Granted as in the foregoing Suit.

CHARLES HAYES ----------Compt)
     vs   (Bill & Injunction
SAMUEL HARRISON----------Deft.)

On petition of Samuel Harris Defendant for a Rehearing in this Cause and Order of Survey &c. and on argument and Reasons appearing to the Court Ordered that a Rehearing of the aforesaid Cause be had at the next Term and that in the meantime the premises be Surveyed and Plotted according to an Entry made in the name of Thomas Batts and according to an Entry made in the name of Jesse Bean on which Said Hayes Grant Issued and also according to the Lines of said Harriss'es Grant and ploted in such manner as to shew how the Lines interfere and that Francis Alexander Ramsey Execute the same.

HENDERSON and COMPANY - Compt)
     vs   (Original Bill
HENDERSON and COMPANY - Deft)

It appearing to the satisfaction of the Court here that Publication heretofore ordered have actually been made in this Suit agreeable to Such Order in the public Gazette of Kentucky, Hagerstown, Knoxville & North Carolina and the Defendants having failed to put in their answer It is ordered that the Bill of the Complainants be taken Pro Confesso and Set for Tryal next Term.

ALEXANDER HAMILTON ------Compt.)
     vs   (Original Bill
JAMES PATTERSON ---------Deft)

On motion of the Counsel for the defendant, It is ordered by the Court here that the Bill of the Complainants be dismissed his failing to enter Sufficient Security agreeable to the Rules and order of this Court at last Term.

(p 207)   JOHN WADDILL   )
              vs   (Bill & Injunction
      ROBERT PATTERSON)

On motion of the Counsel for the defendant It is Ordered by the Court here that the Bill of the Complainant be dismissed his failing to enter Sufficient Security agreeable to the Rules and order of this Court at last Term.

(The above case is marked through ------------Editor's Note)

JOHN WADDILL   )
   vs   (Bill & Injunction
ROBERT PATTERSON)

Agreeable to a Rule of this Court Robert King and James Hubbert Came in and entered themselves Bail for the Deft in five hundred dollars and on motion it is ordered that Copy of depositions of Plaintiff and Defendant Issue for the Plaintiff also Rule for Commissions for Plaintiff and Defendant and Rule for Publication five months hence. _____

SAMUEL WILLSON -------Compt)
        vs   (Bill & Injunction
ELISHA WALLEN --------Deft)

Publication being passed This Cause came on to be heard the 27th of September 1794, and for Reasons appearing to the Court it is ordered to be continued untill next Term

WILLIAM COCKE ----------Compt)
      vs   (Original Bill
RICHARD HENDERSON)   (
    &   (Defts (
COMPANY   )   )

For Reasons appearing to the Court it is ordered that this Cause be Continued.

JOHN TYE -----------Compt.)
     vs   (Bill & Injunction
DAVID REESE ---------Deft.)

It appearing to the Court that (p 208) the Defendant failed to put in his answer agreeable to the Rules thereof. It is therefore ordered by the Court here that the Complainants Bill be taken Pro-Confesso and Set for trial exparte.

AUSTIN SHOAT ---------Compt.)
     vs   (Bill & Injunction
EPHRAM DUNLAP--------Deft.)

Commissions awarded for Plaintiff and Defendant and for Reasons appearing to the Court it is ordered that this Cause be Continued.

WILLIAM GARDNER ----------------------Compt.)
             vs   (Bill & Injunction
MARY LOONEY & the heirs of)   Defts (
BENJAMIN LOONEY Deceased)

For Reasons appearing to the Court it is ordered that the Complainant have Leave to mend his Bill within three months and the Defendants have untill next term to mend his answer.

ALEXANDER MCFARLAND------Compt)
       vs   (Bill & Injunction
ROBERT HOOD ------------Deft)

Rule for commissions for Plaintiff and Defendant and Publication five months hence

(p 209) At a Court of Equity begun and held for the District of Washington at the Court house in Jonesborough on March 17th 1795.
Present the Honourable
      David Campbell &) Esqr Judge of
      Joseph Anderson) Said Court.

WILLIAM BLEVINS ---Compt)
      vs   (Bill & Injunction
JOHN SHELBY -------Deft)

WILLIAM BLEVINS)
   &   (Compts (
OTHERS   )   )
    vs   (
JOHN SHELBY ------Deft)

WILLIAM BLEVINS ----Compt)
      vs   (
JOHN BROWN --------Deft) In pursuance to a former Decree it is ordered by the Court here that Executions Issue for Costs in the foregoing Suits.

Den on Demise of   )
JOHN SHELBY   (
    vs   (Writ of Ejectment
WILLIAM BLEVINS & Others)

Agreeable to a former Decree it is ordered by the Court that an Alias Writ of Possession Issue in favour of John Shelby

CHARLES HAYS ------------Compt)
      vs   (Bill & Injunction.
SAMUEL HARRIS ----------Deft) Rehearing.

On motion of the Counsel for the Defendant it is ordered that order of Resurvey be Renewel and Plats Returned to this Term and for Reasons appearing to the Court it is ordered that this Cause be Continued.

(p 210)   HENDERSON & COMPANY)
                        vs   (Original Bill
                 HENDERSON & COMPANY)

On the 17th day of March 1795 this Cause Came on to be heard the Defendants failing to put in their answer the Complainants Bill being taken Pro Confesso at last Term and the aforesaid Bill being now Read it is ordered by the Court here that this Cause be Continued/

JOHN WADDLE ----------Compt.)
                 vs   (Bill & Injunction
ROBERT PATTERSON ----Deft.)

The same day this Cause came on to be heard and the death of defendant being Suggested, it is ordered by the Court that Scire Facias Issue against the Executors or Administrator to shew Cause why the Injunction shall not be made Perpetual

SAMUEL WILLSON --------Compt)
                 vs   (Bill & Injunction
ELISHA WALLEN ----------Deft.)

This same day this Cause Came on to be heard and Reasons appearing to the Court on affidavit of the Defendant, It is ordered that this Cause shall be open for the examination of Testimony on both sides for five months hence.

WILLIAM COCKE --------Compt.)
                 vs   (Original Bill
RICHARD HENDERSON)   Defts)
& COMPANY   )

For Reasons appearing to the Court it is ordered that this Cause be Continued.

JOHN TYE -------Compt.)
                 vs   (Bill & Injunction
DAVID REES -----Deft.)

The same day this Cause Came on (p 211) to be heard the Complaints Bill being read it is Ordered by the Court here that it be Rendered Perpetual

AUSTIN SHOAT ----------Compt)
                 vs   (Bill & Injunction
EPHRAIM DUNLAP --------Deft.)

The same day this Cause came on to be heard and on motion it is ordered that a Rule for publication of Testimony five months hence and Commissions awarded to take depositions for Plaintiff and Defendant

WILLIAM GARDNER ----------Compt)
   vs   (
MARY LOONEY & the Heirs of) (Original Bill
BENJAMIN LOONEY Decd.)Defts.)

          On motion it is ordered by the Court
here that the Defendants have untill next term to answer plead or Demurr.

ALEXANDER MCFARLAND--------Compt)
   vs   (Bill & Injunction
ROBERT HOOD ------------Deft.)

          On March the 20th 1795 this Cause Came on
to be heard the Plaintiffs Bill and the Defendants answer being read it is
ordered by the Court here that the Plaintiffs Bill of Injunction be Dissolved & that the Respondents have the Benefits of their Judgment at Common
Law.

JOHN CARNEY ------------Compt)
   vs   (
EPHRAIM DUNLAP)   ) Original Bill
 vs   (Defts. (
ANN MOORE)   )

          For Reasons appearing to the Court it is
ordered that this Cause abate as to Ann Moore and on motion the Plaintiff
has leave to amend his Bill.

(p 212)   ROBERT KERR --------Compt)
      vs   (Bill & Injunction
     ALEXANDER MEEK -----Deft)

JOSEPH RENNALDS ----------------Compts)
   vs   (
RUTH TOOL administratrix)) Original Bill
ARCHIBALD ROAN &   (Defts (
JOHN HACKETT administrators(   )
of JOHN TOOL Decd.   )) for Reasons appearing to the
            Court it is Ordered that the
above cause be continued.

JOHN GILLILAND --------Compt.)
   vs   (Bill & Injunction
JOHN SHIRLEY ----------Deft.)

          On motion it is Ordered by the Court here
that a Ducestecun on behalf of the Defendant Issue to James Sevier Clerk
of Washington County Court to bring up the Records Respecting the Caveats
between the Parties and it is agreed to by the parties that the Death of
Either Shall not abate this Suit and for Reasons appearing it is Ordered
that this Cause be continued.

DAVID BOOTH ------------Compt.)
   vs   (
BENJAMIN FORD)   )Original Bill
  &   (Defts (
GARRETT FITZGERALD)   ) Commissions awarded for Plaintiff & De-
          fendant & For Reasons appearing to the

Court it is ordered that this Cause be Continued.

LAWRENCE KETTERING ———————Compt.)
         vs   (Original Bill
JOHN KEYWOOD ——————————Deft)

                                   Commissions awarded for Plaintiff and
Defendant and for Reasons appearing to the Court it is ordered that this
Cause be continued

(p 215)   JAMES BERRY ——————————Compt)
                  vs   (Bill & Injunction
               THOMAS AMIS ——————————Deft)

                                 Rule for Publication five months
hence, Commissions awarded for Plaintiff and Defendant and for Reasons appearing to the Court it is Ordered that this Cause be Continued.

JOHN FEAGAN ——————————————————————Compt)
         vs   (
SAMUEL WILLSON &   )   ) Sci Fa
PETER MCNAIREE Securities(Defts (
for PETER MCCALL   )   (

                                 Scire Facias made known to Samuel
Willson in presence of James Williams and William Berry by Thomas Berry
Sheriff also made known to Peter McNamee in presence of George Moore and
Robert Gwin per Robert Houston Sheriff.

The defendants being Called it is ordered adjudged and decreed that final
Judgment be Entered up against them.

ANDREW GREER Senior ———————Compt)
          vs   (Bill and Injunction
MICHAEL MONTGOMERY ———————Deft)

                               On reading Bill and answer it is Ordered by
the Court here that the Injunction of the Complainant be dissolved and Bill
retained as an Original Bill on the Defendant giving Sufficient Security to
abide by and perform the final Decree of the Court that shall be rendered
thereon, and commissions awarded for Plaintiff and Defendant.

MARTIN ARMSTRONG ——————————Compt.)
         vs   (Bill and Injunction
ANDREW GREER ——————————————Deft.)

                              On reading Bill and answer it is ordered
by the Court here that the In- (p 214) junction of the Complainant be
dissolved, and on motion of the Plaintiffs Attorney the Bill is retained
as an Original Bill, - Exceptions be taken to the Plaintiffs Security it
is further ordered that he give other and better Security and that the Defendant give Security to abide by the decree that shall be finally rendered
thereon.

COTTERAL BAILEY)
      vs   (Bill and Injunction
ANDREW GREER   )

On motion of the Defendants Attorney it is ordered that the Plaintiffs Bill of Complaint be dissolved and on motion of Plaintiffs Attorney it is retained as an original Bill and that the Defendant give Security to abide by the decree that Shall be finally rendered thereon.

(p 215) At a Court of Equity begun and held for the District of Washington at the Court house in Jonesborough the third tuesday in September 1795.

Present the Honourable

David Campbell) Esquires
Joseph Anderson (Judges of
& John McNairy) Said Court.

CHARLES HAYES)
    vs   (Rehearing
SAMUEL HARRIS)

On the 24th and 25th of September 1795 this Cause came on to be heard and on reading bill and answer it is ordered adjudged and Decreed that the former decree made in September 1793 be confirmed, and the Court will advise as to the Costs and it is further ordered that a Writ of Possession issue to Samuel Harris agreeable to his recovery at Common Law for one hundred and eight acres of Lands laying within the line of his patent Grant and without the lines of Charles Hayes's of four hundred acres of Land lying on Lick Creek in Greene County.

HENDERSON and COMPANY)
    against   (Original Bill
HENDERSON and COMPANY)

For reasons appearing to the Court here it is Ordered that this Cause be Continued untill next Term.

JOHN WADDILL)
   agst   (Bill - Injunction
ROBERT PATTERSON)

On motion it is ordered that this Cause be Continued and for reasons appearing to the Court it is also ordered that Scire Facias issue the legal Heirs and representatives of the said Robert Patterson to appear at the next Term and revive ____

(p 216)   SAMUEL WILLSON)
      agst.   (Bill & Injunction
ELISHA WALLEN)

On the 24th of Sept 1795 this Cause Came on to be heard and the following issue being Joined between the parties under the direction of the Court Viz, Whether the lands Claimed by Elisha Wallen by Virtue of his oldest improvement so as to cover or take in the lands Claimed by Samuel Wilson and now in dispute whereupon came the parties aforesaid by their Attornies and also a Jury Viz. 1 Charles McCrae 2 Joseph Brittain 3, John Sevier, 4 Joseph Crouch 5, John Strain, 6 William Medlock 7, John Grinder 8, George Vinwent 9 James Gaines 10, William Evans 11, Robert Rutledge 12, John Morris who being duely impanneled and sworn on their oath do say that the Land Claimed by virtue of the eldest improvement, and as the same was Surveyed and marked out by John Ooulter (Poulter) does cover the Land claimed by Samuel Wilson now in dispute.

WILLIAM COCKE)
   against   (Original Bill
RICHARD HENDERSON & CO.)

               For reasons appearing to the Court it is ordered that this Cause be continued.

AUSTIN SHOAT)
   versus   (Bill & injunction
EPHRAIM DUNLAP)

               For reasons appearing to the Court it is ordered that this Cause be Continued.

WILLIAM GARDINER)
     vs   (Original Bill
MARY LOONEY and the Heirs of (
BENJAMIN LOONEY deceased)

               For reasons appearing to the Court it is ordered that this Cause be Continued and also Commissions awarded for Plaintiff and Defendant.

(p 217)   JOHN CARNEY)
              vs   (Original Bill
           EPHRAIM DUNLAP)

               Ordered by the Court that Scire Facias Issue to the legal Representatives of Ann Moore to appear at next Court to revive.

ROBERT KERR)
   against   (Bill & Injunction
ALEXANDER WEEK)

               This Cause continued by consent and Commissions awarded for the defendant.

JOSEPH RENOLDS)
     vs   )
RUTH TOOL administratrix & (Original Bill
ARCHIBALD ROAN and JOHN (
HACKETT, administrators of)
JOHN TOOL deceased)

               On Reading Bill and answer it is ordered adjudged and decreed that the Bill be dismissed at Costs of Defendants.

(The following case is marked through ----------Editor's Note)

STOCKLEY DONELSON)
     vs   (Bill & Injunction
NATHANIEL HENDERSON)

On motion it is ordered that this Cause be continued untill next term.

(The following case is marked through ----------Editor's Note)

WILLIAM COBB   )
    vs   (Original Bill
WILLIAM CONWAY   (
& JESSEE EVANS   )

For reasons appearing to the Court it is ordered that the Plaintiff have leave to amend his bill, and that George Conway be made a defendant to the Complainants bill and it is also ordered that John and Robert Adams of the State of Virginia be appointed to take the answer of Jessee Evans.

(p 218)   JOHN GILLILAND)
        vs   (Bill and Injunction
               JOHN SHIRLEY)

On the 26th of September 1795 this Cause came on to be heard A Jury impaneled and Sworn Viz, Samuel Wilson, John Criner, John Sims, William Medlock, George Vincent, James Gains William Evans Robert Rutlige, James Morris Elishal Wallen, Garrett Fitzgerald, and James Ryan who being duly sworn to try the following issue of fact, whether John Gilliland or John Shirley or those under whom they Claim, made the first lawfull improvement on the premises in dispute and on argument of Council in behalf of Plaintiff and Defendant it is decreed by the Court here, that the Bill of the Complainant be made perpetual.

DAVID BOOTHE   )
    agt.   (Rehearing
BENJAMIN FORD &   (
GARRETT FITZGERALD)

For reasons appearing to the Court it is ordered that this Cause be continued

LAURENCE KETTERRING)
        (Ketron)   (
    vs   (Original Bill
JOHN CAWOOD   )

This cause continued by consent.

JAMES BERRY   )
    vs   (Bill - Injunction
THOMAS AMIS   )

This Cause continued on affidavit of Defendant and Commissions awarded for defendant.

ANDREW GREER Senr.)
    vs   (Bill & Injunction
MICHAEL MONTGOMERY)

For reasons appearing to the Court, it is decreed that the defendant have the benefitt of his Judgment at law, Bond and Security (p 219) being given according to the directions of the Court and that this Cause be Continued and Commissions be awarded for Plaintiff and Defendant.

MARTIN ARMSTRONG)
  vs   (Bill and Injunction
ANDREW GREER & (
JOHN LETTEN JONES)

On motion of the Attorney for Andrew Greer, one of the Defendants in this Suit it is decreed that he have the benefit of his Judgment at Law on his giving bond and Security to abide by the decree that Shall be finally rendered there on - and it is further ordered that publication be made in the Knoxville Gazette that John Letton Jones appear at next Term and file his answer.

COTTERAL BAILEY)
  vs   (Bill & Injunction
ANDREW GREER)

On motion of the Plaintiffs attorney it is ordered that he have leave to amend his bill.

DAVID WRIGHT)
  vs   (Original Bill
ALEXANDER BAINE)

Ordered that publication be made in the Knoxville Gazette that Alexander Baine the defendant file his answer at next term, and it appearing to the Satisfaction of the Court here that he is not an inhabitant of this Territory it is ordered that Colonel Andrew Lewis, Colo. William McClenihan and Colonel James Barnet or either of them (of the State of Virginia) be appointed commissioners to take the answer of the said Alexander Baine.

RICHARD WOODS)
  vs   (Bill and Injunction
BALT WOODS)
THOMAS WOODS & (
BENJAMIN GIST)

On motion of the Plaintiffs attorney (p 220) it is publication issue to Batt Woods and Thomas Woods to answer at next term, otherwise the Bill will be taken Pro. Confesso.

JOHN FAGAN)
  vs   (
JOHN WOOD) Bill and Injunction
JOHN PRITCHET & (
EDMUND BEAN)

On motion it is ordered, that the Defendants have time untill next term to answer.

RUTH BROWN)
vs (Bill and Injunction
JOHN MCDOWEL)

Ordered that the defendant have leave untill next term to file his answer and do appoint James Greenlee and William Irwin to take his answer.

JOHN CLOWER)
vs (Bill and Injunction
JOHN FEGAN)

Ordered by the Court with the Consent of the parties that this Suit be arbitrated by George Rutlege John Scott, William McCormack and Hugh Montgomery and in case any of the parties Should refuse to Serve as arbitrators the persons that did choose them may call upon any others that they think proper to do the business and then four to meet on the Second thursday in February at Blountville and if they cannot agree they are to choose umpire and their award to be the Rule.

STOCKLEY DONELSON)
vs (Bill & Injunction
NATHANIEL HENDERSON)

On motion it is ordered that this Cause be Continued untill next term

(p 221)   WILLIAM COBB)
vs (Original Bill
WILLIAM CONWAY (
& JESSEE EVANS)

For reasons appearing to the Court it is ordered that the Plaintiff have leave to amend his Bill and that George Conway be made a defendant to the Complainants bill and it is also ordered that John and Robert Adams of the State of Virginia be appointed to take the answer of Jessee Evans.

JOHN GILLILAND)
vs (Scire Facias
JAMES STINSON & (
WILLIAM COX bail)
for JOHN SHIRLEY)

It is ordered by the Court here that Execution issue against the Defendants according to Scire Facias

ANDREW ENGLISH)
vs (Scire Facias
AZARIAH DOLY)
bail for GEORGE (
MARTIN)

It is ordered by the Court here that execution issue against the defendants according to Scire Facias.

(p 222) At a Court of Equity begun and held in the Town of Jonesborough on Friday the eighteenth day of March one thousand Seven hundred and Ninety Six for the District of Washington in the Territory of the United States of America South of the River Ohio

Present the Hona^ble
                  Joseph Anderson, Judge of Said Court.

CHARLES HAYS   )
     vs   (Rehearing
SAMUEL HARRIS)
              For reasons appearing to the Court it is ordered that this Cause be continued, on the same rule made at last Term.

HENDERSON & CO)
     vs   (Continued
HENDERSON & CO)

JOHN WADDILL   )
     vs   (Scire facias is made known to WILLIAM PATTERSON in the
ROBERT PATTERSON) presence of THOS HENDERSON and JOHN MUMPOWER
                              THOS. BERRY Shff.

SAMUEL WILSON)
     vs   (Bill & Injunction
ELISHA WALLEN)

WILLIAM COCKE   )
     vs   (Original Bill
RICHARD HENDERSON & CO)
               For reasons appearing to the Court it is Ordered that the foregoing Causes be continued

AUSTIN CHOAT)
     vs   (Bill & Injunction
EPHRAIM DUNLAP)
              Ordered by the Court that this Cause be continued and that Commissions be awarded for the Defendant.

(p 223)   WILLIAM GARDNER   )
            vs   (Original Bill
       MARY LOONEY and the   (
      Heirs of BENJAMIN LOONEY)
          Deceased   )
                        Ordered by the Court that this Cause be continued and that Commissions be awarded for the Plaintiff and defendant.

JOHN CARNEY   )
     vs   (Original Bill
EPHRAIM DUNLAP and the legal (
Representatives of ANN MOORE deceased)

On motion of the plaintiffs attorney it is order-
ed by the Court here that publication be made in the Knoxville Gazette for
three months to the legal representatives of Ann Moore to appear at next
term and revive otherwise the Bill will be taken Pro confesso and publication the first day of next Term also rule for commissions for Plaintiff and
defendant.

ROBERT KERR)
  agst.   (Bill & Injunction
ALEXANDER MEEK)

     For reasons appearing to the Court it is ordered that this
Cause be Continued - and Commissions awarded for defendants.

DAVID BOOTH)
  vs   (Rehearing
BENJAMIN FORD & (
GARRETT FITZGERALD)

     For reasons appearing to the Court it is ordered that
this Cause be Continued.

LAURENCE KETTERING)
  vs   (Original Bill
JOHN CAWOOD)

     For reasons appearing to the Court it is ordered that
this Cause be continued Commissions (p 224) awarded for Plaintiff & Defendant.

JAMES BERRY)
  vs   (Bill & Injunction
THOMAS AMIS)

     For reasons appearing to the court it is ordered that this
Cause be Continued Commissions awarded for Plaintiff & defendant.

ANDREW GREER Senr.)
  vs   (Bill and Injunction
MICHAEL MONTGOMERY)

     For reasons appearing to the Court it is ordered that
this Cause be continued and that Commissions be awarded for Plaintiff & defendant and also thirty days notice to the defendants attorney to take Testimony

MARTIN ARMSTRONG)
  vs   (Bill & Injunction
ANDREW GREER & (
JOHN LETTON JONES)

     For reasons appearing to the Court it is ordered that
this Cause be continued and that Commissions be awarded for Plaintiff and
Defendant, and it is also ordered that the Plaintiff do proceed within two
terms, otherwise his bill be dismissed.

COTTERAL BAILEY)
  vs   (Bill and Injunction.
ANDREW GREER)

On motion of the defendants attorney it is ordered that he have further time until next term to answer the amended bill.

DAVID WRIGHT)
  vs   (Original Bill
ALEXANDER BAINE)

On motion it is ordered by the Court here that the defendant have further time, until next term (p 225' to file his answer.

RICHARD WOODS)
  vs   (
BATT WOOD) Bill & Injunction
JOHN WOOD & (
BENJAMIN GEST)

It is ordered by Court here that Benjamin Gest file his answer the first day of next term otherwise the bill will be taken confessed as to him and the publication be made in three successive numbers of the Knoxville Gazette, that Batt Wood and Thomas Wood appear at the next term and file their answer, otherwise the bill will be taken as confessed.

JOHN FEGAN)
  vs   (Bill and Injunction
JOHN WOOD)
JOHN PRITCHET (
& EDMUND BEAN)

It appearing to the Court here that the Injunction was prayed to Stay the costs of the complainants own Suit at law it is therefore ordered that the Injunction be dissolved So far as it respects the Costs in the Court below, but that the bill be retained as an original.

RUTH BROWN)
  vs   (Bill & Injunction
JOHN MCDOWELL)

For reasons appearing to the Court it is ordered that this Cause be continued and that Commissions awarded for Plaintiff and defendant

JOHN CLOWER)
  vs   (Bill and Injunction
JOHN FEGAN)

(p 226)   STOCKLEY DONELSON)
       vs   (Bill & Injunction
   NATHANIEL HENDERSON)

It is ordered adjudged and decreed by the Court here that the Plaintiffs bill of Complaint be dissolved and that the defendant have the benefit of his Judgment at law.

WILLIAM COBB)
  vs   (Original Bill
WILLIAM CONWAY)
and OTHERS (It is ordered by the Court that the defendants have further

time untill next term to file their answer.

STOCKLEY DONELSON)
    vs   (Bill and Injunction
JOHN SHIELDS)

    It is ordered that the defendant appear on the first day of the next term and file his answer.

MICHAEL HARRISON)
    vs   (Bill & Injunction
WILLIAM MURPHEY (
& ISAAC THOMAS)

    Ordered by the Court here that James Greenlee, William Irwin and John Henry Stanley Esquires and each of them be impowered by Commission to take the defendants answer and it is further ordered by his Honor that the Complainant give a better prosecution bond for the payment of the Said Murpheys Judgment at Law as well as the Costs of this Suit in case he fail herein, otherwise the bill shall be dismissed at the next term.

(p 227) At a Court of Equity begun and held in the Town of Jonesborough on Friday the thirtyeth day of September one thousand Seven hundred and ninety Six for the District of Washington in the State of Tennessee

Present the Honorable
    John McNairy
    Archibald Roan &
    William Charles Cole Claiborn
Judges of Said Court

CHARLES HAYES)
    vs   (rehearing
SAMUEL HARRIS)

    Ordered that this Cause be continued and that the Court will advise as to the Costs.

HENDERSON and COMPANY)
    vs   (Original Bill
HENDERSON and COMPANY)

JOHN WADDILL)
    vs   (Bill and Injunction
ROBERT PATTERSON)

    Ordered by the Court that the foregoing Causes be Continued.

SAMUEL WILLSON)
    vs   (Bill an Injunction
ELISHA WALLEN)

    The foregoing Cause Compromised by the Complainant and defendant (to wit) the defendant relinquishes to the Complainant the land in dispute and gives up the said Land on the first day of January and pay all Costs except the Complainants attorney and the attendance of the following witnesses (to wit) John Adair, Joseph Bishop John Rice, John Wallen and James Anderson which was made a rule of this Court and Cause ordered to be dismissed accordingly

(p 228)   WILLIAM COCKE   )
                    vs   (Original Bill
          RICHARD HENDERSON and COMPANY)
                              Ordered by the Court that Writ of Subpoena Issue to the defendants to answer the amendments of the Complainants Bill.

AUSTIN SHOAT   )
       vs   (Bill and Injunction
EPHRAIM DUNLAP   )
              Order_ by the Court that this Cause be continued and that Commissions Issue to Plaintiff and defendant

WILLIAM GARDNER   )
       vs   (Original Bill
MARY LOONEY and the heirs   (
of BENJAMIN LOONEY Deceased)
              Ordered by the Court that a Copy of the Amended Bill of the Complainant and writ of Subpoena Issue to the defendants to appear at next Term and answer.

JOHN CARNEY   )
       vs   (Original Bill
EPHRAIM DUNLAP & the heirs   )
of ANN MOORE, deceased   )
              Ordered by the Court that this Cause be Continued and that Commissions Issue to Plaintiff and defendant.

ROBERT KERR   )
       vs   (Bill and Injunction
ALEXANDER WEEK   )

DAVID BOOTHE   )
       vs   (rehearing
BENJAMIN FORDS and   (
GARRETT FITZGERRALD   )
              Ordered by the Court that the foregoing Causes be Continued.

(p 229) SAMUEL KETTRON)
                vs   (Original Bill
         JOHN KEYWOOD   )
                      On the thirtyeth of September 1796 this Cause Came on to be heard and thereupon also came a Jury (to wit) David Reese John Waddle Alexander Nelson, George Nowland, Robert Campbell, James Haygood, Walter Johnson, Alexander Greer, Andrew Greer, David Kincade, Joseph Young and John Weir, who being Sworn well and truly to inquire whether the premises Claimed by the defendants answer are Contained within the lines of the Grant to John Shelton

under which the defendant Claims on their oaths do find that the premises
Claimed by the defendants answer are contained within the lines of the
Grant to John Shelton.

JAMES BERRY)
    vs   (Bill and Injunction
THOMAS AMIS)

        For reasons appearing to the Court it is Ordered that this
Cause be continued and that Commissions Issue to the Defendant.

ANDREW GREER Senr.)
    vs   (Bill and Injunction
MICHAEL MONTGOMERY)

        Ordered by the Court that this Cause be Continued and
that Commissions Issue to Plaintiff and defendant.

MARTIN ARMSTRONG)
    vs   (Bill and Injunction
ANDREW GREER and (
JOHN LETTON JONES)

        Ordered by the Court that this Cause be Continued.

(p 230) COTTERAL BAILEY)
        vs   (Bill and Injunction
    ANDREW GREER Senr)

        The defendant consents to a rule for commiss-
ions on condition that it shall not preclude him from any advantage in the
pleadings or future progress of the Suit and it is Ordered by the Court that
this Saving of advantage shall be mutual.

DAVID WRIGHT)
    vs   (Original Bill
ALEXANDER BAIN)

        The Plaintiffs death Suggested It is Ordered by the Court
that Scire facias Issue to the heirs of the said Alexander Bain to appear at
the next Term and revive.

RICHARD WOODS)
    vs   (Bill & Injunction
BATT WOOD)
THOMAS WOOD & (
BENJAMIN CHEST)

        For reasons appearing to the Court it is ordered that Batt
Wood and Thomas Wood have further time untill next term to file their answer.

JOHN FEGAN)
    vs   (
JOHN WOOD)   Bill and Injunction
JOHN PRITCHETT (
& EDMOND BEAN) Ordered by the Court that John Wood and John Pritchett file

their answer at the next Term otherwise the Plaintiffs Bill will be taken
as confessed.

RUTH BROWN   )
    vs   (Bill & Injunction
JOHN McDOWELL)

               Ordered by the Court that this Cause be continued and that
Commissions Issue to Plaintiff and defendant.

(p 231)   WILLIAM COBB   )
           vs   (Bill & Injunction
   WILLIAM CONWAY & OTHERS)

               John Rhea attorney for the Defendants agrees
to bring in the answer of George Conway at next term on his receiving A Copy
of the Order making of the Said George a party to the Complainants Bill.

MICHAEL HARRISON)
     vs   (Bill & Injunction
WILLIAM MURPHEY (
& ISAAC THOMAS   )

            on Reading Bill and answer It is ordered adjudged and de-
creed that the Plaintiffs Bill be Dissolved and on motion of the Plaintiffs
attorney It is ordered that the Bill be retained as an Original and that a
Copy of this decree shall not Issue to Clerk at Law untill the said William
Murphey shall give bond with sufficient Security with Condition that in case
a decree be made in this Court against the said William Murphey that he shall
refund and pay back all sums recovered at Law and such further sums as shall
or may be decreed for Costs against him on a final determination of this suit

STOCKLEY DONELSON)
    vs   (Bill and Injunction
JOHN SHIELDS   )

           Ordered by the Court that this Cause be Continued

WILLIAM EVANS   )
    vs   (Original Bill
NATHANIEL DAVIS & (
JAMES CHARTERS   )

           Ordered by the Court that this Cause be Continued.

(p 232)   SAMUEL MAY Senr.)
          vs   (
   GEORGE INGLE   ) Original Bill
   HENRY OLDHAM & (
   NANCY OLDHAM   )

           For reasons appearing to the Court It is ordered
that unless Nancy Oldham by Guardian appear at the next term and file her
answer that the Complainants bill be taken as Confessed as to her Self and
It is also further ordered that Alias Subpoena Issue to the other defendants
to appear and file their answers.

JOHN SHARP)
    vs   (Bill & Injunction
JOHN ADAIR)
           Ordered by the Court that this cause be Continued.

EDWARD ERWINE)
    vs   (Original Bill
BENJAMIN ERWINE)
           For Reasons appearing to the Court, It is ordered that
the defendant have further time untill next Term to file his answer.

On the first day of October 1796.
Present the Honorable John McNairy Archibald Roan and William Charles Cole
Claiborn Judges of the Court of Equity for Washington District in the State
of Tennessee when John Carter was duely and Constitutionally appointed Clerk
and Master of said Court, and took the several Oaths required by Law and was
Commissioned as follows,
State of Tennessee Washington District September 1796 ____
Pursuant to the Authority vested in us by the Constitution we have nominated
and appointed John Carter Clerk and Master in Equity for the District aforesaid during his good Behaviour. Given under our (p 233) hands the 1st day
of October in the year 1796.

                    John McNairy
                    Archibald Roan
            William Charles Cole Claiborne.

At a Court of Equity begun and held for the District of Washington in the
Town of Jonesborough on the 31st day of March 1797.

Present the Honorable
              Archibald Roan and
         William Charles Cole Claiborne
Judges of said Court

CHARLES HAYES)
    vs   (Rehearing
SAMUEL HARRIS)
           For reasons appearing to the Court here it is ordered by their
honors that Charles Hayes pay the Costs of the rehearing.

HENDERSON & CO)
    vs   (Original
HENDERSON & CO)
           For reasons appearing to the Court It is Ordered that this
Cause be Continued.

JOHN WADDILL)
    vs   (Bill & Injunction
ROBERT PATTERSON)
           For reasons appearing to the Court It is Ordered that this

Cause be Continued and Publication of Testimony after five months.

(p 234)   WILLIAM COCKE   )
                        vs   (Original Bill
              RICHARD HENDERSON & CO)

                    It appearing to the Court that the Several defendants Contained the Complainants Bill of Complaint have not filed their Answers of Complaint. It is therefore order_ by their honors that Publication be inserted in the Knoxville Gazette and also in the Gazettes Published by Hodge and Willis at Halifax North Carolina for three weaks Successively that the several defendants appear at the next Term and file their answers otherwise the Complainants Bill will be taken Pro Confesso._____

AUSTIN SHOAT   )
              vs   (Bill of Injunction
EPHRAIM DUNLAP   )

                  For reasons appearing to the Court it is ordered that this Cause be continued and publication of testimony after five months.

WILLIAM GARDENER   )
                        vs   (Original Bill
MARY LOONEY and the heirs (
of BEN LOONEY decd.   )

                  For reasons appearing to the Court it is ordered that this Cause be continued and that Commissions issue to plaintiff and defendant.
On motion of the Complainants attorney and reason shewn, it is also ordered that the Complainant have leave to withdraw the depositions by him filed.

JOHN CARNEY   )
              vs   (
EPHRAIM DUNLAP and)
the heirs of   (
ANN MOORE   )

                  For reasons appearing to the Court it is ordered That this Cause be continued and that Commissions issue to plaintiff & defendant Publication of testimony after five months.

(p 235)   ROBERT KEER   )
                        vs   (Bill & Injunction
              ALEXANDER MEEK)

                  For reasons appearing to the Court it is ordered that this Cause be Continued, and Commissions issue to plaintiff and defendant. Publication five months hence.

DAVID BOOTHE   )
              vs   (
BENJAMIN FORD &   (rehearing
GARRET FITZGERALD)

                  For reasons appearing to the Court it is ordered this

Cause be continued.

LAWRENCE KETTERON)
vs (Original Bill
JOHN KEYWOOD)

For reasons appearing to the Court it is ordered that this Cause be Continued, and Commissions issue to plaintiff and defendant. Publication after five months.

JAMES BERRY)
vs (Bill & Injunction
THOMAS AMIS)

For reasons appearing to the Court it is ordered that the Complainant and Defendant have leave to amend Bill and answer the Complainants Waives the privelege of amending.

ANDREW GREER Sr.)
vs (Bill & Injunction
MICHAEL MONTGOMERY)

For reasons appearing to the Court it is ordered that publication of testimony be made on the fifth day of next term unless Cause be shewn to enlarge the rule and that commissions issue to plaintiff and defendants.

(p 236)   MARTIN ARMSTRONG)
vs (Bill & Injunction
ANDREW GREER &)
JOHN LETTON JONES)

On motion of the defendant Andrew Greers attorney it is ordered by the Court here that this Cause be dismissed for the want of prosecution as required by an order made in March Term 1796.

COTTRAL BAILEY)
vs (Bill & Injunction
ANDREW GREER)

Refered by consent of plaintiff and Defendant as appears by written agreement filed.

DAVID WRIGHT)
vs (Original Bill
ALEXANDER BAIN)

On motion of the defendants attorney it is ordered by the Court here that the Complainant or his representatives appear at next Term and prosecute this suit otherwise it will be dismissed.

RICHARD WOODS)
vs (
BATT WOOD - THOS. WOOD) Bill & Injunction
& (
BEN. GEST)For reasons appearing to the Court it is ordered

that Batt Wood have time untill next Term to file his answer.

JOHN FEGAN)
vs (
JOHN WOOD) Bill & Injunction
JOHN PRITCHETT (
&)
EDMOND BEAN) Dismissed by Consent of parties and John Wood assumes the
Costs.

(p 237) RUTH BROWN)
vs (Bill and Injunction
JOHN MCDOWELL)
The Defendants death suggested. Ordered by Court that
this Cause be Continued.

WILLIAM COBB)
vs (Original Bill
WILLIAM CONWAY & Others)
Ordered by Court that this Cause be continued and that
Commissions issue to plaintiff and Defendant.

MICHAEL HARRISON)
vs (
WILLIAM MURPHEY) Bill & Injunction
& ISAAC THOMAS)
It is ordered by the Court that this Cause be continued.

STOCKLEY DONALSON)
vs (Bill & Injunction
JOHN SHIELDS)
Ordered by the Court that this Cause be continued

WILLIAM EVANS)
vs (
NATHANIEL DAVIS &) Original Bill
JOHN CHARTERS exrs)
Order by the Court that cause be Continued.

SAMUEL MAY Sen.)
vs (
GEORGE INGLE) Original Bill
HENRY OLDHAM & (
NANCY OLDHAM)
For reasons appearing to the Court it is ordered that the
other defendants have further time (p 238) to file their answer.

JOHN SHARP)
vs (Bill & Injunction
JOHN ADAIR)
Ordered by the Court to be continued.

EDWARD ERWIN)
    vs   (Original Bill
BENJAMIN ERWIN)

        It is ordered by the Court that this Cause be continued and that Comissions issue to plaintiff & defendant

JOHN BLEVINS)
    vs   (Bill & Injunction
JOHN SHELBY Senr.)

        On motion of the complainants Attorney it is ordered by the Court that he have issue to plaintiff and Defendant.

JOHN ALLISON & Others   )
        vs   (Original Bill
ROBERT ALLISON & FRANCIS HODGE)

        Ordered that this Cause be continued and that Comissions issue for plaintiff and defendant.

JOHN LAUGHLIN)
    &   (
ROBERT CRAIG) Original Bill
    vs   )
JOHN VANCE)

        It is ordered by the Court that unless the defendant appear at next Term and file his answer the Bill of the Complainant will be taken pro Confesso.

(p 239) At a Court of Equity begun and held for the district of Washington in the town at Jonesborough, on the 29th day of September 1797.

Present the Honorable,
        Archibald Roan
      William Charles Cole Claiborne
        & Howel Jatham
esqrs., Judges of Said Court.

HENDERSON & CO.)
    vs   (Original Bill
HENDERSON & CO.)

JOHN WADDELL)
    vs   (Bill & Injunction
ROBERT PATTERSON)

WILLIAM COCKE   )
    vs   (Original Bill.
RICHARD HENDERSON & CO)

AUSTIN SHOAT)
    vs   (Bill & Injunction
EPHRAIM DUNLOP)

For reasons appearing to the Court it is ordered that the foregoing Causes be continued &c.

WILLIAM GARDNER	)
vs	(Original Bill
MARY LOONEY & the heirs	)
of BENJAMIN LOONEY decd	)

It is ordered by the Court that this Cause be Continued and Commissions issue for the plaintiff and defendant.

JOHN CARNEY	)
vs	(Original Bill
EPHRAIM DUNLOP & the	)
heirs of ANN MOORE decd	(

(p 240)   ROBERT KEER   )
                    vs   (Original Bill
          ALEXANDER WEEK)

DAVID BOOTHE	)
vs	(Rehearing
BENJAMIN FORD &	)
GARRETT FITZGERALD	)

Ordered by the Court that the foregoing Causes be Continued.

LAWRENCE KETTRON)
     vs   (Original Bill
JOHN KEYWOOD   )

It is ordered by the Court to be continued and commissions to issue to the plaintiff & defendant

JAMES BERRY)
     vs   (Bill &Injunction
THOMAS AMIS)

Ordered by the Court to be continued.

ANDREW GREER Sr.   )
     vs   (Bill & Injunction
MICHAEL MONTGOMERY)

COTTERAL BAILEY   )
     vs   (Original Bill
ANDREW GREER Senr)

For reasons appearing to the Court it is ordered that the foregoing Causes be continued and that commissions issue for Plaintiff and Defendant.

DAVID WRIGHT   )
     vs   (Original Bill
ALEXANDER BAIN)

It is ordered by the Court that this Cause be continued.

(p 241)   RICHARD WOODS)
            vs   (Bill & Injunction
    BATT WOOD)
    THOMAS WOOD & (
    BENJAMIN GEST)

                 On argument of Counsel for Plaintiff and Defendant
It is ordered adjudged and Decreed by the Court that the Complainants Bill
of Complaint be taken Pro confesso as to Batt Wood.

RUTH BROWN)
    vs   (Bill and Injunction
JOHN MCDOWELL)

           For reasons appearing to the Court here it is ordered that
Scire facias issue against Ann McDowell widow Colonel John Carson & William
Whitson Executors of Said John McDowell deceased to appear at the next term
and revive.

WILLIAM COBB)
    vs   (Original Bill
WILLIAM CONWAY & others)

           For reasons appearing to the Court it is ordered
that the plaintiff and defendant have leave untill next Term to amend Bill
and answer and that Commissions issue to plaintiff & defendant.

MICHAEL HARRISON)
    vs   (
WILLIAM MURPHEY (Bill & Injunction
& ISAAC THOMAS)

STOCKLEY DONELSON)
    vs   (Bill & Injunction
JOHN SHIELDS)

WILLIAM EVANS)
    vs   (Original Bill
NATHANIEL DAVIS &(
JAMES CHARTERS)

(p 242)   SAMUEL WAY Senr.)
           vs   (
    GEORGE INGLE) Original Bill
    HENRY OLDHAM & (
    NANCY OLDHAM)

EDWARD ERWINE)
    vs   (Original Bill
BENJAMIN ERWINE)

           For reasons appearing to the Court it is ordered that the
five foregoing causes be continued untill next Term.

JOHN SHARP)
   vs   (Retained as an Original Bill.
JOHN ADAIR)

           On argument of Counsel for Plaintiff and Defendant, It is Ordered adjudged and decreed by the Court here that the Complainants Bill of Injunction be Dissolved and on argument of Complainants attorney it is also ordered that his bill be retianed as an Original.

JOHN BLEVINS)
   vs   (Bill and Injunction
JOHN SHELBY)

           It is Ordered by the Court that this Cause be continued.

JOHN ALLISON & Others)
      vs   (Original Bill
ROBERT ALLISON &   (
FRANCIS HODGE   )

           on the 26th of September 1797 this Cause was compromised by the parties at Mutual Costs which was ordered by the Court to be entered of Record.

(p 243)   JOHN LAUGHLIN)
      & ROBERT CRAIG (
          vs   (Original Bill
      JOHN VANCE)

           It is Ordered by the Court that this Cause be Continued untill next term.

JOHN JOHNSTON)
   vs   (Bill and Injunction
MOSES CARRICK)

           It is ordered by Court that this Cause be continued and that Commissions issue to Plaintiff and Defendant.

JOHN WILLSON   )
   vs   (Original Bill
ANDREW & JACOB EMERT)

           Compromised by the parties the plt. pays his own attorney and all other Costs except one half of the Sheriffs fee and half of Copying of the Bill, the Ballance assumed by Henry Harklerhode which was ordered to be made a rule of this Court.

(p 244) At a Court of Equity begun and held for the District of Washington in the town of Jonesborough on the 15th day of March 1798.

Present the honorable
          Archibald Roan)esqrs. Judges
          Howell Tatham & (of said Court.
          David Campbell)

HENDERSON & CO.)
   vs   (Original Bill
HENDERSON & CO.)

For reasons appearing to the Court it is ordered that this cause be continued.

JOHN WADDILL)
vs (Bill & Injunction
ROBERT PATTERSON)

For reasons appearing to the Court it is ordered that this Cause be Continued and set for trial at next Term.

WILLIAM COCKE)
vs (Original Bill
RICHARD HENDERSON & CO.)

It is ordered by the Court that publication be made in the Knoxville Lexington and Salisberry Gazettes; for the defendants to appear at next Term and file their answer otherwise the Complainants Bill be taken pro confesso.

AUSTIN SHOAT)
vs (Bill & Injunction
EPHRAIM DUNLOP)

For reasons appearing to the Court it is ordered that this Cause be continued & set for trial at next Term.
Publication of Testimony after five months and that Commissions issue for Plaintiff and defendant.

(p 245) WILLIAM GARDNER)
vs (Original Bill
MARY LOONEY and the heirs (
of BENJAMIN LOONEY decd.)

For reasons appearing to the Court it is ordered that this Cause be continued and Commissions issue to Plaintiff and Defendant. Publication of Testimony on the first Monday of August next.

JOHN CARNEY)
vs (Original Bill
EPHRAIM DUNLOP)

For reasons appearing to the Court it is Ordered that this Cause be Continued and that Publication be made in the Knoxville Gazette that the heirs of Ann Moore appear at the next term and file their answers otherwise the Compt. bill will be taken Pro Confesso - also Commissions issue to Plaintiff and Defendant.

ROBERT KEER)
vs (Bill and Injunction
ALEXANDER MEEK)

It is Ordered by the Court that this Cause be Continued untill next term and that Commissions issue for Plaintiff and Defendant.

DAVID BOOTHE)
vs (rehearing
BENJAMIN FORD and (
GARRET FITZGERALD)

On reading Bill and answer and reasons shewn it is Ordered by the Court that the issues of facts filed by the Defendants be tried at the next term, and that Commissions issue for Plaintiff and Defendant.

(p 246) LAURENCE KETIRON)
    vs   ) Original Bill
  JOHN KEYWOOD)

On argument of Counsel for Plaintiff and Defendant, it is Ordered by the Court here, that the Demurer be so far Sustained that the defendant shall not be Compelled to answer those Complainants entering Claims in the entry office prosecuting Caveats against the defendant, Orders & proceedings of Sullivan Court thereon But that the Complainant shall never theless have leave to hold up those parts of the bill for Supporting any Equitable Titles as far as he can Support the same by other proof than the defendants confession also ordered to be continued and that Commissions issue to Plaintiff and Deft.

JAMES HERRY)
  vs   (Bill & Injunction
THOMAS AMIS)

The death of the defendant suggested in abatement Therefore it is ordered by the Court that this Cause be Continued until next Term.

ANDREW GREER Sen.)
  vs   (Bill & Injunction
MICHAEL MONTGOMERY)

For reasons appearing to the Court it is ordered that this Cause be Continued and that Commissions Issue for plaintiff and defendant.

COTTERAL BAILEY)
  vs   (Original Bill
ANDREW GREER Sr.)

Rule of reference set aside and it is ordered by the Crowd that publication of testimony be made on the first Monday of August next commissions for plaintiff and defendant.

(p 247) DAVID WRIGHT)
    vs   (Original Bill
  ALEXANDER BAIN)

Ordered that this Cause be continued.

RICHARD WOODS   )
  vs   (Bill & Injunction
BATT WOOD, THOMAS WOOD)
& BENJAMIN GEST   )

For reasons appearing to the Court it is ordered that the Judgment pro Confesso against Batt, be set aside & that his answer be received and filed, also that Commissions issue for plaintiff and defendant.

RUTH BROWN)
vs (Bill & Injunction
JOHN MCDOWELL)

Ordered by the Court to be Continued.

WILLIAM COBB)
vs (Original Bill
WILLIAM CONWAY & Others)

On motion of Counsel for the defendants it is ordered that time be given them untill next Term to file their answers.

MICHAEL HARRISON)
vs (Bill & Injunction
WILLIAM MURPHEY (
& ISAAC THOMAS)

Ordered that this Cause be Continued and that Commissions issue to the Complainant.

STOCKLEY DONELSON)
vs (Bill and Injunction
JOHN SHIELDS)

Ordered by the Court to be continued.

(p 248)   WILLIAM EVANS)
vs (Original Bill
NATHANIEL DAVIS and (
JAMES CHARTERS)

on reading Bill and answer and on argument of counsel it is ordered adjudged and decreed by the Court here, It is ordered that the demurrer be sustained and that the Bill of the Complainant be dismissed.

SAMUEL WAY Senr.)
vs (Original Bill
GEORGE INGLE (
HENRY OLDHAM &)
NANCY OLDHAM

On argument of Counsel for the plaintiff and defendant it is ordered by the Court that this Cause be continued, & that publication be made in the Knoxville Gazette in three successive numbers that Henry Oldham do file his answer at the next Term, otherwise the Bill of the Complainant will be taken pro confesso and that a commission issue to take this answer before the presiding Judge of the County Court of ------

EDWARD ERWINE)
vs (Original Bill
BENJAMIN ERWINE)

on motion of the plaintiffs attorney it is ordered that this Cause be continued and that Commissions issue to plaintiff & defendant.

JOHN SHARP)
vs (Original Bill
JOHN ADAIR)

It is Ordered by the Court that this Cause be Continued and that Commissions issue to Plaintiff and defendant.

(p249)   JOHN BLEVINS)
               vs   (retained as an Original Bill.
     JOHN SHELBY)

On Reading Bill and answer and on argument of Counsel for Plaintiff and defendant it is ordered adjudged and Decreed by the Court here that the Complainants Injunction be dissolved and that his bill be retained as an Original.

JOHN LAUGHLIN)
& ROBERT CRAIG (
     vs   (Original Bill
JOHN VANCE)

It appearing to the Satisfaction of the Court that the defendant hath failed to put in his answer agreeable to a rule made at March term 1797, It is therefore ordered by the Court here that the Bill of the Complainant be taken Pro Confesso.

JOHN JOHNSTON)
    vs   (Bill & Injunction
MOSES CARRICK)

It is ordered that this Cause be continued untill next Term.

THOMAS KING)
    vs   (
BENONI CALDWELL (Original Bill
JOEL GILLENWATERS (
& JOHN HALL)

For reasons appearing to the Court it is ordered by the Court that this Cause be Continued and that Commissions issue to plaintiff and defendant.

WILLIAM CHRISTMAS)
    vs   (Original Bill
NATHANIEL and SAMUEL (
HENDERSON)

Ordered by the Court to be Continued & that the defendants have time (p 250) untill next Term to file their answer.

MICHAEL MONTGOMERY)
    vs   (Bill & Injunction
WILLIAM BURK)

Ordered by the Court to be continued & that the defendant have untill next Term to file his answer.

AGNES TORBETT)
    vs   (Original Bill
ALEXANDER TORBETT)

Ordered by the Court to be continued and that Commissions

issue to plaintiff and defendant.

SAMUEL VANCE)
        vs   (Bill and Injunction
JOHN BEARD   )
                Dismissed by Written agreement.

JOHN MILLIKEN)
        vs   (Bill & Injunction
JOHN SMITH   )
                Ordered by the Court that this Cause be continued and that
the defendant have untill next Term to file his answer.

ANDREW GREER   )
        vs   (Sci fa made know in presence of M. Rhea
JAMES GAINS,Bail for (and Geo. Vincent.
MARTIN ARMSTRONG   )   T. Shelby Shf.

                Being solemnly called and having failed to appear, it
is ordered by the Court that Judgment go against said Jas. Gains according
to Scire facias.

(p 251) At a Court of equity begun and held for the District of Washington
in the town of Jonesborough on the 17th Day of September in the year 1798.

Present the honorable
                Archibald Roane) esqrs.
                & David Campbell)

HENDERSON & COMPANY)
        vs   (Original Bill
HENDERSON & COMPANY)
                It is ordered by the Court that this Cause be Continued.

JOHN WADDELL   )
        vs   (Bill & Injunction
ROBERT PATTERSON)
                It is ordered by the Court that this Cause be Continued
and that the issues of fact made up in this cause be filed

WILLIAM COCKE   )
        vs   (Original Bill
RICHARD HENDERSON & CO)
                For reasons appearing to the Court It is ordered
this Cause be continued and that publication extend only to the Knoxville
Gazette

AUSTIN SHOAT   )
        vs   (Bill and Injunction
EPHRAIM DUNLAP   )

It is ordered by the Court that this Cause be continued untill next Term.

WILLIAM GARDINER)
vs (Original Bill
MARY LOONEY & the heirs (
of BENJAMIN LOONEY decd)

Ordered by the Court that this Cause be continued untill next Term " that the issues of fact made up be filed.

(p 252)   JOHN CARNEY)
vs (Original Bill
EPHRAM DUNLOP and heirs (
of ANN MOORE decd.)

It is ordered by the Court that this Cause be continued, and publication be made in the Knoxville Gazette that the heirs and legal representatives of Ann Moore appear at the next term and file their answers otherwise the bill of the Complainant will be taken pro confesso.

ROBERT KEER)
vs (Bill & Injunction
ALEXANDER WEEK)

It is ordered by the Court that this Cause be continued and that Commissions issue to plaintiff and Defendant.

DAVID BOOTHE)
vs (rehearing
BENJAMIN FORD & (
GARRET FITZGERALD) It is ordered by the Court that this Cause be Continued and that Commissions issue for Plaintiff and

Defendants

LAURENCE KETTRON)
vs (Original Bill
JOHN KEYWOOD)

This cause was dismissed by the Complainants Attorney.

JAMES BERRY)
vs (Bill and Injunction
THOMAS AMIS)

This cause was referred by written agreement filed.

(p 253)   ANDREW GREER)
vs (Bill and Injunction
MICHAEL MONTGOMERY)

This Cause was dismissed by consent of Plaintiff and Defendant each pays his own Costs, and the said Michael Montgomery relinquishes his Judgment obtained at Common law which is Complained of in the Complainants Bill of Complaint and that the said Andrew Greer be entitled to receive back all sums of money which he has paid to any person, in pursuance of the said judgment at Common law.

COTTRAL BAILEY)
      vs   (retained as an Original
ANDREW GREER)

        By consent of plaintiff and defendant It is ordered by the
Court that this Cause be refered to Landon Carter, Nathaniel Taylor, John
Carter & David McNabb and their award to be a rule of this Court.

DAVID WRIGHT)
      vs   (Original Bill
ALEXANDER BAIN)

        For reasons appearing to the Court it is Ordered that this
Cause be continued and that a Commission issue to James Tapacot and _____
McClenahan of _____ County Virginia empowering them or either of them to
take the answer of the Defendant Alexander Bain; and it appearing to the
Satisfaction of the Court that the Complainant has deceased since the Commencement of this suit, and his administrators appearing at this Term in
open Court were admitted to revive and that Commissions issue To plaintiff
and Defendant.

(p 254)   RICHARD WOODS)
              vs   (
           BAT WOOD)
           THOMAS WOOD and (Bill & Injunction
           BENJAMIN GEST)

        For reasons appearing to the Court it is or-
dered that Cause be Continued and that a D___ tecum issue to the Clerk
of Greene County Court, to bring up the depositions filed in his office in
a Caveat had and tried between the parties in the said County Court of Greene
also publication of Testimony at this day and that the issues of fact made
up between the parties be filed.

RUTH BROWN)
      vs   (Bill & Injunction
JOHN MCDOWELL)

        For reasons appearing to the Court it is ordered that this
Cause be continued and revived against William Whitson Executor of the said
John McDowell deceased and that Commissions issue to plaintiff and defend-
ant.

WILLIAM COBB)
      vs   (Bill & Injunction
WILLIAM CONWAY & Others)

        For reasons appearing to the Court it is ordered
that this Cause be continued a time untill next Term for Jessee Evans one
of the defendants to file his answer to the amended Bill of the Complainant
and also that a Commission issue to John Adams Senr. John Adams Junr. or
either of them of Wythe County Virginia empowering them to take the answer
of the said Jessee Evans.

MICHAEL HARRISON)
    vs (
WILLIAM MURPHEY (Retained as an Original
& ISAAC THOMAS)

      By consent of the plaintiffs (p 255) and Defendants attorney it is ordered by the Court that this Cause be Continued.

STOKELY DONELSON)
    vs (Bill and Injunction
JOHN SHIELDS)

      on reading Bill and answer it is ordered adjudged and decreed by the Court that the Complainants Bill of Injunction be dissolved.

SAMUEL WAY Senior)
    vs)
GEORGE INGLE (Original Bill.
HENRY OLDHAM (
and NANCY OLDHAM)

      For reasons appearing to the Court it is ordered that this Cause be Continued and that unless Nancy Oldham answer by her guardian Joshua Cox, her husband at the next term the Bill of the Complainant will be taken pro confesso as to herself.

EDWARD ERWINE)
    vs (Original Bill
BENJAMIN ERWINE)

      The death of the Complainant suggested, It is Ordered by the Court that Scire facias issue to the legal representatives to revive.

JOHN SHARP)
    vs (Retained as an Original.
JOHN ADAIR)

      It is ordered by the Court that this Cause be continued and that Commissions issue to plaintiff and Defendant.

JOHN BLEVINS)
    vs (retained as an Original
JOHN SHELBY)

      By the Court it is ordered that this (p 256) Cause be continued and by consent of Complainant and Defendant it is agreed that the issues of fact be made up and tried at next Term, and that commissions issue to plaintiff and defendant.

JOHN LAUGHLIN)
& ROBERT CRAIG)
    vs (Original Bill
JOHN VANCE)

      the Complainants Bill of Complaint being taken pro confesso at March Term 1798 and being finally settled at this by the parties it is therefore Ordered by the Court to be Dismissed.

JOHN JOHNSON)
vs (Bill and Injunction
MOSES CARRICK)

Ordered by the Court that this Cause be Continued and that Commissions issue to plaintiff and defendant.

THOMAS KING)
vs (
BENONI CALDWELL) Original Bill
JOEL GILLENWATERS (
& JOHN HALL)

Ordered by the Court to be continued and that Commissions issue to plaintiff and Defendant.

WILLIAM CHRISTMAS)
vs (Original Bill
NATHANIEL and SAMUEL HENDERSON)

Ordered by the Court that this Cause be continued, and that Nathaniel Henderson be and is hereby appointed guardian for Samuel Henderson, and that they have untill next Term to file their answer.

(p 257) MICHAEL MONTGOMERY)
vs (Bill & Injunction
WILLIAM BURKE)

Ordered by the Court that the defendant have untill next Term to file his answer and it appearing to the satisfaction of the Court that the defendant is not an inhabitant of this government it is therefore ordered that a Commission to John Hunt and Joshua Stockton of Fleming County State of Kentuckey empowering them to take the answer of the said William Burke.

AGNES TORBETT)
vs (Original Bill
ALEXANDER TORBETT)

JOHN MILIKEN)
vs (Bill and Injunction
JOHN SMITH)

ROBERT COILE)
vs (Bill & Injunction
THE HEIRS OF WILLIAM (
INGRAM decd) For reasons appearing to the Court it is Ordered
that the foregoing Causes be continued untill next Term and that Commissions issue for plaintiffs and Defendants.

JOHN COULTON)
vs (Bill & Injunction
RICHARD MITCHELL & (
THOMAS HAUGHTON) Ordered by the Court that a subpoena to answer and copy

of Bill issue to the defendants.

(p 258) WILLIAM SKILLERN)
        vs   (Bill and Injunction
    NICHOLAS HAWKINS)

               Ordered by the court to be continued and that commissions issue to plaintiff & defendant.

WILLIAM P. CHESTER)
      vs   (Bill and Injunction
DAVID STEWART)

               Ordered by the Court that an alias Subpoena issue to the Sheriff of Knox County.

JOHN YANCY)
     vs   (Original Bill
JAMES REED)

               Ordered by the Court that the Defendant have untill next Term to answer.

It is ordered by the Court that David Deaderick of Washington County, John Williams of Sullivan County, Thomas Jackson of Hawkins County and Landon Carter of Carter County be and are hereby appointed Commissioners of affidavits for the Counties aforesaid respectively.

Ordered by the Court that James Roddye of Jefferson County be and is hereby appointed guardian for Lewis Russell a minor son of George Russell deceased for the purpose of bringing a suit in equity.

(p 259) At a Court of Equity begun and held in the town of Jonesborough for the District of Washington in the State of Tennessee on the 14th day of March 1799.
Present the Honorable
        Archibald Roane
        David Campbell and
        Andrew Jackson
Esquires Judges of said Court.

HENDERSON & COMPANY)
      vs   (Original Bill
HENDERSON & COMPANY)

JOHN WADDLE)
    vs   (Bill and Injunction
ROBERT PATTERSON)

               It is ordered by the Court the foregoing Causes be Continued untill next Term.

WILLIAM COCKE)
     vs   (Original Bill
RICHARD HENDERSON & COMPANY)

For reasons appearing it is therefore order-
ed by the Court that this Cause be continued and that Publication in the
Knoxville Gazette be renewed.

AUSTIN SHOAT   )
    vs   (Bill and Injunction
EPHRAIM DUNLAP)

        On motion and reasons shewn it is Ordered by the Court
that this Cause be continued and set for tryal at next term also Publication of Testimony four months hence.

WILLIAM GARDNER   )
    vs   (Original Bill
MARY LOONEY & the heirs   (
of BENJAMIN LOONEY deceased)

        For reasons appearing to the (p 260) Court
it is Ordered that this Cause be continued and the issues of fact made up
under directions of the Court be filed and Commissions for Plaintiff and
defendant also Publication of Testimony five days previous to next Term.

JOHN CARNEY   )
    vs   (Original Bill
EPHRAIM DUNLOP & the   (
Heirs of ANN MOORE decd)

        For reasons appearing to the Court it is Ordered
that this Cause be Continued untill next term and that Commissions Issue
to Plaintiff and defendant.

ROBERT KEER ------Compt.)
    vs   (Bill & Injunction
ALEXANDER MEEK ---Deft.)

        For reasons appearing to the Court it is ordered
that this Cause be continued untill next term and Commissions issue to the
Defendant.

DAVID BOOTHE ------Compt)
    vs   (rehearing
BENJAMIN FORD &) Defts)
GARRET FITZGERALD)   )

        On the 14th day of March 1799 the foregoing Cause
came on to be tryed when also Came a Jury (towit) Jessee Pain, Christopher
Taylor, Jacob Brown, Joseph Young, Isaac White, James Hay, Andrew Greer,
Thomas Hughes, Timothy Acoff, Samuel Wilson, Michael Montgomery & James
Galbreath to well and truly try the following issues of fact, towit, Whether any and what were the conditions on which David Boothe put into the hands
of Benjamin Ford a negro girl named Bet, whether a tender of the sum money
Thirty four pounds five shillings (p 261) Virginia money was made by David Boothe or any other person for him to Garret Fitzgerald or Benjamin Ford
and if any at what time & what is the values of the services of the negro
girl Bet by the year, on their Oaths do find and say lst we find the negro

wench was put into the hands of Benjamin Ford for the payment of Thirty
four pounds five shillings Virginia money to be paid by David Boothe
2nd we find no Lawfull tender to be made by said Boothe or any other person for him.
3d we find the yearly Services of said wench to be worth the interest of
said thirty four pounds five shillings and paying taxes for said wench
and finding her Clothes.
And on arguments of Counsel Learned in the Law for complainant and Defendant it is Ordered adjudged and Decreed that this Honorable court
that the Bill of the Complainant be Dismissed with Costs.

JAMES BERRY --------Compt.)
      vs   (Bill & Injunction
THOMAS MIS --------Deft.)

                        For reasons appearing it is Ordered by the
Court that this be continued untill next Term _ and that the rule of reference made at last Term be set aside and that Commissions issue for
Plaintiff and deft twenty days notice to the adverse parties for taking
depositions Publication of Testimony on the first day of the next Term.

COTTERAL BAILEY ---Compt.)
      vs   (retained as an Original
ANDREW GREER -----Deft.)

                        For reasons appearing it is Ordered by the
Court that this Cause be Continued untill next term and that the rule of
reference made at the last term be set aside also Commissions issue for
Plaintiff & defendant. (p 262) And that Publication of Testimony five
days previous to next term.

DAVID WRIGHT ------Compt.)
      vs   (Original Bill
ALEXANDER BAIN -----Deft.)

                        For reasons appearing to the Court it is there
fore Ordered that this Cause be continued and Publication be inserted in
the Knoxville Gazette that the defendant Alexander Baine file his answer on
the first day of next Term otherwise the Bill of the Complainant will taken
pro confesso, it is also ordered by this Honorable Court that a Commission
issue to James Tapscot and _____ McClenahan of Botte tourt County and State
of Virginia empowering them and each of them to take the answer of Alexander
Baine.

RICHARD WOODS --------Compt.)
      vs   (
BATT WOOD   )   (Bill & Injunction
THOMAS WOOD   ((
    &   (Defts (
BENJAMIN GEST)   )

                        For reasons appearing it is ordered by the
Court that this Cause be Continued untill next term a resurvey being prayed
by the Defendants on the premises in dispute which was granted accordingly
and that Daniel Rawlings be and is hereby appointed Surveyor to perform the
same.

RUTH BROWN ------Compt.)
     vs   (Bill & Injunction
JOHN MCDOWELL ----Deft.)

                   For reasons appearing it is ordered by the Court that this Cause be continued and that Commissions issue for Plaintiff and deft. a written agreement filed.

(p 263) WILLIAM COX ------Compt.   )
           vs   (Original Bill
        WILLIAM CONWAY & Others Deft.)

                   For reasons appearing it is Ordered by the Court that this Cause be Continued untill next term and that Commissions issue for Plaintiff and defendant.

MICHAEL HARRISON ---Compt)
     vs   (
WILLIAM MURPHEY)   (retained as an Original
& ISAAC THOMAS) Defts)

                   For reasons appearing it is ordered by the Court that this Cause be Continued.

SAMUEL MAY Sr.------Compt   )
       vs   (Original Bill
GEORGE INGLE,HENRY OLDHAM)   (
& NANCY OLDHAM ----------(Defts)

                   Nancy Oldham one of the Defendants in this Cause having failed to enter her appearance agreeable to an Order of Publication made at Sept. 1798 It is therefore Ordered that the bill of the Complainant be taken Pro Confesso as herself and it appearing to Satisfaction of the Court that Henry Oldham another deft. is not an inhabitant of this State it is therefore ordered that a publication be inserted in the Knoxville Gazette or Nashville in two Successive numbers that unless he appear at the next Term and file his answer the Bill of the Complainant will be taken Pro Confesso as to him and that Commissions issue for Plaintiff and deft.

(p 264) EDWARD ERWINE ----Compt.)
          vs   (Original Bill
       BENJAMIN ERWINE---Deft.)

                   Joseph McMinn Executor of the last will and Testament of Edward Erwine deceased by his Attorney comes into Court and revives this suit, it is therefore Ordered by the Court to be continued untill next Term.

JOHN SHARP---------Compt.)
     vs   (retained as an Original
JOHN ADAIR -------Deft)

                   For reasons appearing it is Ordered by the Court that this Cause be Continued untill next Term, and Commissions issue to Plaintiff and Defendant Publication of Testimony on the first day of February next, issue of fact made up under the directions of the Court and ordered to be filed.

JOHN BLEVINS ------Compt.)
       vs   (retained as an Original
JOHN SHELBY ------Deft.)

                    For reasons appearing it is ordered by the Court that this cause be Continued untill the next Term and commissions issue to Complainant and Defendant.
Publication of Testimony Six months hence issues of fact made up under the directions of the Court and Ordered to be filed.

JOHN JOHNSTON ------Compt)
        vs   (Bill & Injunction
MOSES CARRICK ------Deft)

                    For reasons appearing it is ordered by the Court that this Cause be continued untill the next Term and Commissions issue to Complainant and defendant. Publication of Testimony five months hence.

(p 265)   THOMAS KING ----Compt   )
                vs   (
            BENONI CALDWELL)   ) Original Bill
            JOEL GILLENWATERS(Defts (
            & JOHN HALL   )   )
                    For reasons appearing it is ordered by the Court this Cause be continued untill the next Term and Commissions issue to Plaintiff and Defendant.

WILLIAM CHRISTMAS------Compt   )
           vs   (Original Bill
NATHL. & SAML. HENDERSON-Deft.)

                    For reasons appearing it is ordered by the Court that the Defendants have leave untill next Term to amend their answers.

MICHAEL MONTGOMERY -------Compt.)
        vs   (retained as an Original.
WILLIAM BURKE ------------Deft.)

                    It is ordered by the Court that this Cause be Contd. untill the next Term.

AGNESS TORBETT ------------Compt.)
        vs   (Original Bill
ALEXANDER TORBETT----------Deft.)

                    On motion for a rule of reference which was not admited. Ordered by the Court that this Cause be continued untill next Term and that Commissions issue to Compt. and defendant.
Publication of Testimony five months hence.

JOHN MILIKEN -----------Compt.)
        vs   (Bill & Injunction
JOHN SMITH-------------Deft.)

                    For reasons appearing it is ordered by the Court that this Cause be contin- (p 266) ued untill next Term and that Commissions issue to the Complainant.

WILLIAM CHRISTMAS------------ Compt)
            vs   (Original Bill
NATHL. & SAMUEL HENDERSON ---Deft)

The defendants having failed to Enter their appearance agreeable to a rule heretofore made by this Honorable Court, it is therefore Ordered that the bill of the Complainant be taken Pro confesso. on motion of the Defendants attorney, it is Ordered by the Court that the Rule pro Confesso be set aside and answer filed on motion it is order_ by the Court they have leave untill next Term to amend their Answer.

MICHAEL MONTGOMERY --------Compt.)
            vs   (Bill & Injunction
WILLIAM BURKE ------------Deft.)

On the 15th day of March 1799 this Cause Came on to be tryed, Bill and answer having read it is Ordered by the Court that the Injunction of the Complainant be Dissolved and on motion the bill retained as an Original and leave to amend the same.

AGNESS TORBETT -----Compt)
            vs   (Original Bill
ALEXANDER TORBETT---Deft.)

For reasons appearing it is ordered by the Court that this Cause be continued untill next Term and that Commissions issue to Complainant and defendant publication of Testimony on the first day of the next Term.

JOHN MILIKEN --------Compt)
            vs   (Bill & Injunction
JOHN SMITH ----------Deft)

(p 267) ROBERT KILE - Compt   )
            vs   (
        the Heirs of WILLIAM) Defts (To perpetuate Testimony
        INGRAM Deceased   (   )

For reasons appearing it is ordered by the Court the foregoing Causes be Continued untill next Term and that Commissions issue to Plaintiff and defts.

JOHN COULTER ---------------Compt)
            vs   (Bill & Injunction
RICHARD MITCHELL &)   (
THOMAS HOUGHTON) Defts   )

Ordered by the Court that this Cause be Continued untill the next term for the answer of Thomas Houghton.

WILLIAM SKILIERN ---------Compt.)
            vs   (Bill & Injunction
NICHOLAS HAWKINS ---------Deft.)

For reasons appearing it is Ordered by the

by the Court that this Cause be Continued untill next Term and that Commissions issue to Plaintiff and deft. Publication of Testimony on the first day of the next term.

WILLIAM P. CHESTER ----------Compt.)
           vs   (Bill & Injunction
DAVID STUART ----------------Deft.)

                            This Cause Dismissed per verball Order of the Complainant the Defendant assumes Costs.

JOHN YANCY ----------Compt.)
        vs   (Original Bill
JOHN REED -----------Deft.)

                  For reasons appearing it is ordered by the Court that this Cause be Continued (p 268) untill next Term and that the Deft have leave untill next Term to amend his Answer.

MARK MITCHELL -----------Compt.)
       vs   (Bill & Injunction
MICHAEL MONTGOMERY -----Deft.)

            On reading bill and answer and argument of Counsel for Plaintiff and deft. the Court Ordered this Cause to be continued untill next term, and that Commissions issue to Plaintiff and deft. Publication of Testimony the first Saturday of next Term.

JAMES KING -----------Compt.)
        vs   (Bill & Injunction
JOHN OVERTON &)
DAVID ALLISON)   Defts.)

           On reading bill and answer and on argument of Counsel for Plaintiff and Defendant it is Ordered by the Court that the injunction of the Complainant be Dissolved and that the Defendant have the benefit of his Judgment at Law.

JOHN SEVIER JUR.------Compt.)
      vs   (
SAMUEL JACKSON)   ) Bill & Injunction
JOHN B. EVANS & (Defts. (
DAVID ALLISON)   )

         For reasons appearing it is ordered by the Court that this Cause be Continued untill the next Term and that a Commission issue to the Mayor of the Corporation of George Town State of Maryland to take the answer of Saml. Jackson one of the Defendants also one other Commission to the Mayor of City of Philadelphia to take the answer of John B. Evans Deft.

(p 269) LAURENCE HORN ------Compt.)
         vs   (Bill & Injunction
      THOMAS GIBBONS------Deft.)

          For reasons appearing it is Ordered by the Court that this Cause be Continued and that the Defendant have untill next Term to file his answer.

WILLIAM RUSSELL & Others --Compt)
      vs   (
The Heirs of RICHARD & WILLIAM) (Bill & Injunction
CASWELL Deceased & against   (Defts.)
JOSEPH BLAIR   ))

               For reasons appearing it is Ordered
by the Court that this Cause be Continued and the Defendants have untill
next Term to answer.

BENJAMIN CULBIRTH --------------Compt.)
      vs   (
ELIZABETH DOTSON &)   ) Bill & Injunction
NATHL. TAYLOR admrs) Defts   (

               On reading bill and answer and on ar-
gument of Counsel for plaintiff and Defendant it is Ordered by the Court
that the injunction of the Complainant be Dissolved and on motion it is also
Ordered the bill be retained as an Original.
On the 27th of April 1799 the above Cause Dismissed per written Order of the
Compt.

THOMAS KING & others ------Compt.)
      vs   (Bill & Injunction
JAMES DANIEL --------------Defts.)

               on reading bill and answer and argument
of Counsel for Complainants and defendants it is Ordered by the Court the
the Complainants injunction be Dissolved on motion the bill retained as an
Original.

(p 270)   (This page is blank in book ----------Editor's Note)

(p 271) At a Court of Equity begun and held in the Town of Jonesborough for
the District of Washington in the State of Tennessee on the 12th day of September 1799.

Present the Honorable
          Archibald Roane)
          David Campbell & (Esquires &c.
          Andrew Jackson)

HENDERSON & CO)
    vs   (Original Bill
HENDERSON & CO)
               For reason appearing it is ordered by the Court that this
Cause be continued untill next Term.

JOHN WADDLE ----------Compt.)
      vs   (Bill & Injunction
ROBERT PATTERSON ------Deft.)

               Ordered by the Court that this Cause be Cont'd.

WILLIAM COCKE ---------------Compt.)
      vs   (Original Bill
RICHARD HENDERSON & CO.------Deft)

                              This Cause Dismissed per verball Order
of the Complainant.

AUSTON SHOAT ------------Compt.)
      vs   (Bill & Injunction
EPHRAIM DUNLAP---------Deft.)

                         On the 13th of September 1799 this Cause Came
to be heard, bill and answer being read it is Ordered adjudged and Decreed
by the Court that the Injunction of the Complainant be Dissolved and bill
Dismissed.

WILLIAM GARDNER ---------------Compt.)
         vs   (
MARY LOONEY & the Heirs of   (Original Bill
BENJAMIN LOONEY, Deceased   )

                        On the 12th day of (p 272) September
1799 the foregoing cause came to be Tried whereupon Came a Jury (towit) Ben
jamin Holland, Daniel Hamlen John Bayless, Joseph Crouch, Thomas Prater, Dav
id Russell, John Wear, John Newman, Richard Mitchell, Isaac Tipton, Samuel
Wood & Robert Alison who being impanneled and sworn to well and truly try
the following issues of Fact (towit) whether a contract took place between
the said Benjamin Looney in his life time and the said William Gardner concerning said Land as stated in the Complainants Bill and if a Contract did
take place what it was.
2nd Whether said William Gardner has paid the Purchase money Stipulated to
be paid by him for Land and if the whole has not been paid what part; and
if all or any part has been paid in what manner at what time and to whom,
has the same been paid.
3rd If any Contract was made between the said Benjamin in his life time and
the Said Williams as stated in the Complainants Bill, whether the Same has
been revoked by the said Benjamin and Williams on their Oaths do say. 1st
we find that a Contract did take place between the Complainant William Gard
ner & Benjamin Looney as Stated in the bill of Complaint 2nd We find that
the Purchase money was paid by Gardner to Benjamin Looney.
3rd We find that no revocation ever was made between the parties.
              For reasons appearing it is Ordered by the Court that this Cause
be Continued untill next Term for a final Decree.

JOHN CARNEY ------------------Compt.)
      vs   (
EPHRAIM DUNLAP &   )   ) Original Bill
Heirs of ANN MOORE Decd.) Deft. (

                       The Heirs of Ann (p 273) Moore Deceas
ed having failed to enter their appearance agreeable to an Order of Publication made at September Term 1798 it is therefore Ordered by the Court that
the Bill of Complainant be taken Pro Confesso as to them.

ROBERT KEER ------Compt.)
      vs   (Bill & Injunction
ALEXANDER WEEK----Deft.)

          For reasons appearing it is ordered by the Court that this Cause be continued untill next Term and that Commissions issue to Complainant and defendant.

JAMES BERRY ------Compt.)
      vs   (Bill & Injunction
LUCY AMIS ---------Deft.)

          For reasons appearing it is ordered by the Court that this cause be continued untill next Term and that Commissions issue to Plaintiff and defendant Publication of Testimony.

COTTERAL BAILEY -------Compt.)
      vs   (retained as an Original
ANDREW GREER -----------Deft.)

          on the 14th day of September 1799 this Cause Came on to be tried bill and answer being read the defendant having demured to part of the Complainants Bill and on motion that the demurer be sustained the Court took an advisare as to the demurer issue of fact on the Plea to be tried at the next Term Commissions to both parties, Publication of Testimony five months hence.

DAVID WRIGHT --------Compt.)
      vs   (Original Bill
ALEXANDER BAINE--------Deft.)

          For reasons appearing it (p 274) is ordered by the Court that this Cause be continued untill next Term, Commissions issue to Compt. and defendant thirty days notice to be given for taking depositions in the State of Virginia.

RICHARD WOODS -------Compt.)
      vs   (Bill & Injunction
BALT WOOD   )   )
THOMAS WOOD & (Defts   )
BENJAMIN GIST)   )

          A Survey of the premises in dispute being prayed for by the Defendants Attorney it is Ordered by Court that it be granted and that Daniel Rawlings on the part of the defendants and James Galbreath on the part of the Complainant be and are hereby appointed and empowered to perform same and make return to the next Term and Commissions issue Compt. and defendants

RUTH BROWN ------------Compt.)
      vs   (Bill & Injunction
JOHN MCDOWELL ---------Deft.)

          For reasons appearing it is ordered by the Court that this Cause be continued untill the next Term Publication of Testimony five months hence and forty days notice to the adverse party for taking depositions in the state of North Carolina.

WILLIAM COBB -----Complainant)
                vs   (Original Bill
WILLIAM CONWAY & others-Defts.)

            For reasons appearing it is Ordered by the
Court that this Cause be continued & Commissions issue to Compt. and defts.
thirty days notice for taking depositions in the State of Virginia Publication of Testimony five months hence.

(p 275) MICHAEL HARRISON -------Compt)
                vs   (retained as an Original
            WILLIAM MURPHEY)   )
            & ISAAC THOMAS) Defts   )
                        For reasons appearing it is ordered
by the Court that this Cause be Continued untill the next Term.

SAMUEL MAY Senr.-------Compt)
            vs   (
GEORGE INGLE   )   ) Original Bill
HENRY OLDHAM & (Defts   (
NANCY OLDHAM   )   )
            Henry Oldham one of the Defendants in this Cause
not having entered his appearance agreeable to an Order of Publication made
at March Term 1799 it is therefore Ordered by the Court that the bill of the
Complainant be taken pro confesso as to himself. Publication of Testimony
five months hence.

JOSEPH McMINN Exr. of)   )
EDWARD ERWINE Decd. (Compt (
) Original Bill
            vs   (
BENJAMIN ERWINE -------Deft)
                On the 13th day of September 1799 this Cause
Came to be heard bill and answer being read in presence of Counsel for Complainant and defendant the Court say they will advise of this Cause untill
next Term.

JOHN SHARP ---------Compt.)
            vx   (retained as an Original
JOHN ADAIR ---------Deft.)
                For reasons appearing it is ordered by the Court
that this Cause be Continued untill next Term and Commissions issue to Plaintiff and Defendant. Publication of (p 276) Testimony on the first day of
February next issues of fact made up under the directions of the Court and
Ordered to be filed.

JOHN BLEVINS -------Compt.)
            vs   (retained as an Original
JOHN SHELBY --------Deft.)
                For reasons appearing it is ordered by the
Court that this Cause be Continued untill the next Term and Commissions issue
to Complainant and Defendant. Publication of Testimony Six months hence,
issues of fact made up under the directions of the Court and ordered to be
filed.

JOHN JOHNSTON----------- Compt.)
          vs   (Bill & Injunction
MOSES CARRICK --------Deft.)

                        For reasons appearing it is Ordered by the Court that this cause be Continued untill the next Term and Commissions issue to Complainant and defendant. Publication of Testimony five months hence.

THOMAS KING --------Compt)
        vs   (
BENONI CALDWELL)   ) Original Bill
JOEL GILLENWATER (Defts (
& JOHN HALL   )   )

                        For reasons appearing it is ordered by the Court that this Cause be continued untill next Term, and Commissions issue to Plaintiff and Defendant.

WILLIAM CHRISTMAS--------Compt.)
          vs   (Original Bill
NATHL. & SAML. HENDERSON--Defts)

                        For reasons appearing it is Ordered by the Court that the Defendants have leave untill next Term to amend their answers.

(p 277) MICHAEL MONTGOMERY --- Compt)
            vs   (retained as an original
         WILLIAM BURKE --------Deft)

                        It is Ordered by the Court that this Cause be contin'd. untill the next Term.

AGNESS TORBETT----------Compt.)
        vs   (Original Bill
ALEXANDER TORBETT-------Deft.)

                        On motion for a rule of reference which was not admitted, Ordered by the Court that this Cause be Continued untill next Term and that Commissions issue to Compt. and defendant. Publication of Testimony five months hence.

JOHN MILIKEN ------Compt.)
       vs   (Bill & Injunction
JOHN SMITH---------Deft.)

                        For reasons appearing it is Ordered by the Court that this Cause be Continued untill the next Term and that Commissions issue to the Complainant.

ROBERT KILE --------Compt.)
       vs   (To perpetuate Testimony
RICHARD MITCHELL) Defts (
& THOMAS INGRAM (   )

                        Ordered by the Court that this Cause be Continued untill next Term and that Commissions issue to the Complainant.

```
JOHN COULTER ----------Compt )
          vs              ( Bill & Injunction
ROBERT MITCHELL & ) Defts )
THOMAS HOUGHTON    (       )
```
For reasons appearing it is Ordered by the
Court that this Cause be Continued untill the next Term and that a Commission issue to Judge Walton of the State of (p 278) Georgia empowering him
to receive upon Oath the answer of Thomas Haughton and in the meantime a
Publication be inserted in two successive numbers of the Knoxville Gazette
that Unsless Thomas Houghton one of the Defendants enter his appearance at
the next term, the bill of the Complainant will be taken Pro Confesso as to
him and that a Survey of the Premises in dispute be made and Joseph Cobb
is hereby appointed & empowered to perform the same.

```
WILLIAM SKILLERN --------Compt.)
          vs              ( Bill & Injunction
NICHOLAS HAWKINS --------Deft. )
```
For reasons appearing it is ordered by the
Court that this Cause be continued untill next Term and Commissions issue
to Compt. & deft., thirty days notice to the adverse party for taking depositions in the State of Kentuckey also twenty days in Washington County State
of Virginia. Publication of Testimony five months hence.

```
JOHN YANCY ----------Compt )
          vs              ( Original Bill
JAMES REED ----------Deft )
```
For reasons appearing it is Ordered by the Court
that this Cause be Continued untill the next Term and Commissions issue to
Complainants and defendants/ Publication of Testimony on the first day of
next Term.

```
MARK MITCHELL ----------Compt.)
          vs              ( Bill & Injunction
MICHAEL MONTGOMERY -----Defts.)
```
For reasons appearing it is ordered by the
Court that this cause be Continued untill the next Term and Commissions issue to the Complainant.

```
(p 279)  JOHN SEVIER - Jnr --Compt )
              vs              ( Bill & Injunction
        SAML. JACKSON  )      )
        JOHN B. EVENS & ( Defts (
        DAVID ALLISON  )      )
```
This cause dismissed per verball Order
of the Complainant, September the 3d 1799.

```
LAWRENCE HORN -----Compt )
          vs          ( Bill & Injunction
THOMAS GIBBONS-----Deft. )
```
For reasons appearing it is Ordered by the Court

that this Cause be continued and that the defendant have time until the fourth day of next Term to answer.

WILLIAM RUSSELL & Others ----------Compt)
              vs   (
The Heirs of WILLIAM & RICHARD)   )Bill & Injunction
CASWELL Deceased &   ((
    against   (Defts)
JOSEPH BLAIR   )   )

                                 Ordered by the Court that this Cause be Continued and Joseph Blair one of the Defendants have leave untill the first day of the next Term to file his answer otherwise the bill of the Complainant will be taken Pro Confesso and that Publication be inserted in the Knoxville Gazette that the other defendants appear on the first day of the next term and file their answers otherwise the bill of Complaints will be taken Pro Confesso as to them.

THOMAS KING & Others ------Compt.)
          vs   (returned as an Original
JAMES DANIEL --------------Deft.)

                                For reasons appearing to the Court it is Ordered that this Cause be Dismissed with Costs.

(p 280)   JAMES REED --------Compt)
              vs   (
        JOHN ADAMS &)   (Original Bill
        JACOB SOOMAN)   Defts)

                               For reasons appearing it is Ordered by the Court that this Cause be Continued untill the next Term.

ROBERT ALLEN-----------Compt)
          vs   (Bill & Injunction
ARCHIBALD BLACKBURN--Deft)

                        The defendant having failed to enter his appearance agreeable to the rules of this Court it is therefore ordered by the Court that the bill of Complainant be taken Pro confesso.

JOHN PITNER-----------Compt.)
          vs   (Bill & Injunction
ROBERT & THOMAS RODGERS-Deft.)

                     Bill and answer being read and on arguments of Counsel for Complainant and defendant it is O rdered by the Court that the Injunction of the Complainant be Dissolved and on motion of the Complainants Attorney it is Ordered by the Court that the bill be retained as an Original and the Defendant Robert Rodgers have the benefit of his Judgment at Law on his giving bond with Sufficient Security to pay back the money. Should the Complainant hereafter recover on his said bill, Commissions for Complainant and defendant.

ROBERT ALISON---------Compt)
          vs   (Original Bill
ISAAC SHELBY   )   )
WILLIAM HUGHES & (Defts)
ELIZABETH HUGHES)   ) For reasons appearing it is ordered by the Court

that this cause be continued untill the next Term and that Alias Subpoena
issue against William & Elizabeth Hughes the other Defendants.

(p 281)   THOMAS KING------Compt.)
                 vs   (Bill & Injunction
           JOHN SMITH -------Deft.)
                                    For reasons appearing it is ordered by the
Court that this Cause be Continued untill next Term and Alias Subpoena issue
against the Defendant to Hawkins County.

ALEXANDER NELSON ------Compt.)
                 vs   (Bill & Injunction
PHILIP NORTH ----------Deft.)
                                    For reasons appearing it is Ordered by the Court
that this Cause be continued and Publication be inserted in the Knoxville and
Winchester Gazettes that the defendant appear here on the first day of the
next Term and file his answer, otherwise the bill of the Complainant will be
taken Pro confesso.

Ordered by the Court that the following notices shall be given to the Adverse
parties of the time and place of taking Testimony on all Commissions hereafter
issued unless where it may be otherwise specially directed. In the State of
Tennessee directed. In the State of Tennessee twenty days. In the State of
Kentuckey Thirty days in the State of Virginia Forty days in the State of
North Carolina Forty days in the State of South Carolina Forty days in the
State of Maryland Forty five days in the State of Pennsylvania Fifty days.

(p 282)   (This page is blank in the book-------Editor's Note)

                              1788
(p 283)   State of North Carolina

   At a Superior Court of Law and Equity began and held in the Court house of
Washington County for the District of Washington this 15th day of February
1788 present The Honorable David Campbell Esquire Judge.

Ordered that Francis Alexander Ramsey Esqr. be appointed Clerk to this Court,
who took the Oath necessary to be taken for the qualification of public Officers and the oath of Office and entered into and acknowledged his bond with
John Tipton and James Stuart Esquires his Securities in the sum of Two thousand pounds Current money payable to the Judges of this Court and their Successors in office with Condition as the Law directs.

Be it remembered that Joshua Duncan personally appeared in Court, and acknowledged himself to be indebted unto the people of this State in the Sum of
one hundred pounds Current money, to be levied of his goods and chattles lands
and Tenements to the use of the people of the said State. Yet upon this Condition that he do appear at the next Court to be holden for this District to
prosecute on behalf of the State against Ezekiel Beard & Henry Chambers.

Be it remembered that Ezekiel Beard Henry Chambers and Richard White personally appeared in Court and severally acknowledged themselves indebted to the people of this State that is to say the said Ezekiel Beard and Richard White in the sum of one hundred pounds and the said Henry Chambers and Richard White in the sum of one hundred pounds current money of their respective goods and chattels lands and Tenements to be levied to the use of the people of this State.

Yet upon this Condition that the said Ezekiel Beard, and Henry Chambers do personally appear at the next Court to be holden for this District to answer what shall then and there be objected against them.

(p 234) Ordered that the Court be adjourned till Court in Course.

At a Superior Court of Law begun and held for the District of Washington in the Court house in Jonesborough the 15th day of August 1788.

Present the Honorable David Campbell esqr. Judge.

Proclamation was made for all Sheriffs and Coroners within this District to make return of all process in their hands, and for all Justices of the peace within this District to make return of all Recognizances by them taken Whereupon Edmund Williams Sheriff for the County of Washington returned upon the Venire facias to him directed for that County that he summoned Robert Love, John Hammer, Joshua Kelley, William Cox, Robert Allison, John Tipton, James Stuart, Alexander Matthews, William Nelson, John Strain, John Campbell, Elijah Cooper, Abedingo Inman, John Wear & Robert Rodgers

BENJAMIN COBB-----plt.)
    against   (In case upon an Appeal.
EDWARD CALLAHAM--Deft.)

    on the motion of the deft. by his attorney It is Ordered that a Commission be awarded directed to the Justices of the county of Washington in Virginia to examine and take the depositions of his Witnesses in this Cause.

    John Hunt Sheriff of Hawkins County having failed to return a Venire facias for the said County Therefore it is considered by the Court that the said John Hunt make his fine with the people of this State by the payment of fifty pounds Current money unless he shall appear at the next Court and shew cause to the contrary.

George Rutledge Sheriff of Sullivan County having failed to return a Venire facias for the said County (p 225) therefore it is considered by the Court that the said George Rutledge make his fine with the people of this State by the payment of fifty pounds Current money unless reasons hereafter shall appear to the Contrary.

James Richardson Sheriff of the County of Greene having failed to return a Venire facias for that County Therefore it is considered by the Court that the said James Richardson make his fine with the people of this State by the payment of fifty pounds Current money, unless reasons hereafter shall appear to the Contrary.

Ordered that Archibald Rowan Esqr. be appointed Attorney to prosecute on behalf of the State

Ordered that the Court be adjourned till tomorrow morning.

Saturday August the 16th 1788 the Court met according adjournment.

William Sharp Esqr. produced a License to practice as an Attorney in the several Courts within this State with a Certificate of his qualification from the Clerk of Morgan District, whereupon he is admitted to practice in this Court.

Ordered that the Court be adjourned till Monday morning ten Oclock.

Monday the 18th day of August 1788, Court met according to adjournment,
Present the Honble Samuel Spencer) Esquires
                    &   (Judges
         David Campbell)

The Sheriff for the County of Greene returned upon Venire facias to him directed for that County that he had Summoned Adam Dunwoody, James Rodgers Henry Earnest, George Doherty, Alexander Pritherow, (p 286) Isaac Taylor Joshua Gist, James Hubbert, John McNabb, Abraham Denton, John Newman, Abraham McCoy, Elisha Baker, William Nelson, Joseph Conway, Alexander Outlaw, Alexander Wilson, David Russell, David Rankin, Major Temple & John Gist. The Sheriff of Sullivan that he had Summoned John Whitcraft, Samuel McCorkle Francis Berry, Jesse Vauter, Jacob Joab, Christian Truesett, William Rhea, Dillen Blevins, John Cox, and Isaac Hicks and the Sheriff of Hawkins County returned that he had summoned Lewis Widener Thomas Amiss and Samuel Currey.

John McNairey Esquire produced a License to practice as an attorney in the Several Courts within this State with a Certificate from the Clerk of the Court for the District of Salisbury that he has taken the Oath's necessary for his qualification as an Attorney whereupon he is admitted to practice in this Court.

Adam Dunwoody foreman Robert Love, Joshua Kelley, John Hammer, William Cox, Robert Allison, John Tipton, James Stuart Alexander Matthews, William Nelson, Elijah Cooper, Robert Rodgers, Alexander Wilson, David Russell, John Whitcraft, Samuel McCorkle, Francis Berry, Jesse Vauter, Christian Truxwell William Rhea Dillen Blevins, John Cox, Isaac Hicks and Samuel Currey who being elected and sworn a Grand Jury of Inquest for the body of this District were charged and withdrew from the bar to consider of their presentments.

EDMUND WILLIAMS -----plt.)
      vs   (
JOHN ADAIR ----------deft.)
               On the motion of the deft. It is ordered that a Commission be awarded him to South Carolina.

Ordered that the Court be adjourned till morrow morning ten O'clock

(p 287) Tuesday morning the 19th day of August 1788. The Court met according to adjournment.

William Sharpe produced in open court a Commission from the honble Samuel Spencer and David Campbell Esqrs. Judges for the District of Washington appointing David Allison Master and Clerk in Equity who produced a Certificate that he had filed bonds with the Secretary agreeable to the Act of Assembly in that case made which was accepted by the honorable Court at Salisbury in March Term 1788 as appears from a copy of the Record from said Court and he having taken the Oath of Allegiance to the State of North Carolina and the oath of office in this Court.
It is therefore Ordered that the said David Allison be admitted as Master and Clerk of the Court of Equity for this District and that notice thereof be given to the said District.

William Cocke Esqr. produced a License to practice as an Attorney in the several Courts within this State and having taken the Oath of Allegiance to the said State & the Oath of Office he is admitted to practice.

James Rees produced a License to practice as an Attorney in the Several Courts within this State having taken the Oath of Allegiance and the Oath of Office he is admitted to practice.

Archibald Rowan Esqr resigned the appointment made by this Court for him to prosecute on behalf of the State. Whereupon William Sharpe Esqr. is appointed in his room.

John Strain, John Campbell, Abednigo Inman and John Wear of Washington County James Rogers Henry Earnest, George Doherty Alexander Pritherow Isaac Taylor, Joshua Gist, James Hubbart, John McNabb, Abraham Denton, Abraham McCoy, Elisha Baker, William Nelson, Joseph Conway, Alexander Outlaw (p 288) David Rankin, Major Temple, and John Gist of Greene County Jacob Jobb of Sullivan County, Lewis Widener and Thomas Amiss of Hawkins County being legally summoned to attend this and they having been called but failing to appear, It is therefore considered by the Court that they be fined for such failure according to the act of assembly in such Case made & provided.

Ordered that James Denton a Constable be appointed to attend upon the Grand Jury who was qualified for that purpose.

EBENEZER FAIN ---appellee)
    against   (Upon an appeal from a Judgment
JOHN NOWLAND------appellant) of the County Court of Washington obtained by the
                         Appellee against the appellant the 4th day of August 1788.

This day came the Appellant by his Attorney and thereupon came also a Jury (towit) David Russell, William Nelson, Samuel Currey, Christian Shultz, William Hues, Pharioh Cobb, Jonathan Tipton, Ebenezer Scroggs John Hunter, William Hall, Joshua Greene and James Davis who being elected and

sworn they hath to speak upon the issue Joined and the Appellee being called
but failing to appear it is therefore ordered that he be non suit and that
the Appelant recover against the appellee his Costs by him in this behalf
expended.

ELIZABETH LOONEY--Appellant)
      against   (Upon an appeal
AGNESS GRAY------ appellee)

                           For reasons appearing to the Court. It is Or-
dered this appeal be continued till the next Court.

PETER MCCAUL -----appellant)
      against   (Upon an appeal from the Judgment of the County
JOHN LEWIS -----appellee) Court of Sullivan.

(p 289) The appellant being called but not appearing on the motion of the
Appellee by his Attorney it is ordered that he be non pros'd.

JONATHAN PUGH administrator of)   )
the Estate of SIMON BUNDY   (appellee (
       against   )   (Upon an appeal from a Judgment of
JAMES EDDEN---------------------------appellant) the County Court of Washington
                                obtained by the Appellee against
the Appellant the ____ day of May 1788.
                         It appearing to the Court that the Trans-
cript of the record in this cause had not been returned fifteen days previous
to the commencement of this term, It is therefore ordered that this Appeal be
dismissed and that Judgment of the Inferior Court be confirmed.

Ordered that the Court be adjourned till tomorrow morning ten Oclock.

Wednesday morning August the 20th 1788 The Court met according to adjournment.

EDMUND WILLIAMS----plt.)
   against   (
JOHN ADAIR -------deft.)
                     Ordered that a Commission issue to take the depositions
of Witnesses in this Cause to Chesterfield County South Carolina.

John and Simon Summers failing to appear according to the Condition of their
Recognizance, tho they were solemnly called, It is therefore Ordered that it
be forfeited.

Joshua Duncan, Ninian Hoskins, William Wilson and John Arnold failing to appear
according to the condition of their respective Recognizance, tho' solemnly called It is therefore Ordered that the said Recognizance be forfeited.

(p 290)   THE STATE OF NORTH CAROLINA----plt.)
           against   (Upon an Indictment for petit
        PETER DOHERTY,alias MCGUIRE   (Larceny.
        alias ROCK--------------------deft)
                        This day came the Attorney for the

State and the deft. in his proper person and the Indictment is read to him. Whereupon he says that he is not guilty in manner and form as in the Indictment is alledged and of this he puts himself upon the County and the Atto. for the State doth the same.

James Richardson Sheriff of Greene, George Rutledge Sheriff of Sullivan John Hunt Sheriff of Hawkins who was fined for non attendance, upon affidavit of the reasons thereof, It is Ordered that each of their fine be remitted.

```
JOHN DUM on the Demise of)   )
SAMUEL HARRISS ----------)pt.(
        against            ) In Ejectment
RICHARD FAIN ----------deft. )
```
On the motion of Christian Shultz he is admitted deft. in this suit in room of sd. Richard Fain and thereupon by W. Avery his Atto. comes and defends the force and injury when &c and pleads the General issue Confesses Lease entry and ouster in the declaration supposed & agrees to insist on the title only at the trial.

```
THE STATE OF NORTH CAROLINA-----plt. )
        vs                            ( Upon an Indictment for petit Larceny
MARGARET RICHEY----------------deft. )
```
This day came the Atto. for the State and the deft. by her Atto. and thereupon came also a Jury to wit, William Nelson, David Russell, Samuel Currey, John Newman, David Hughes, Robert Young, Christopher Taylor, Henry Miller, Peter Parkison, Robert Blackburn, Nicholas Foo's and Hosea Rose who being elected tried and sworn the truth to speak upon the issue Joined upon their Oath do say that the said deft is guilty in manner and form as the atto. for the (p 291) State in his Replication hath alledged, Therefore it is considered by the Court that the said deft. receives ten lashes at the publick whiping post by the hour of four Oclock this afternoon and to remain in custody of the Sheriff until the Costs in this prosecution are paid

The Grand Jury came into Court and presented an Indictment against Elijah Isaacs "A true bill" An Indictment against John SevierJun. and Thomas Conway "A true Bill"

```
THE STATE OF NORTH CAROLINA) plt )
        against                  ( on an Indictment for petit Larceny
PETER DAHERTY als.MCGUIRE ) deft.(
als. ROCK                  (      )
```
This day came the Atto. for the State and the deft. by his Atto. and thereupon Came also a Jury to wit, William Nelson, David Russell, Samuel Currey, John Newman, David Hughes, Robert Young, Christopher Taylor, Henry Miller, Peter Parkison, Robert Blackburn, Nicholas Foos, & Hosea Rose who being elected tried and Sworn the truth to speak upon the issue Joined upon their oath do say that the said deft. is guilty in manner and form as the Atto. for the State in his Replication hath alledged. Therefore it is considered by the Court that the said deft. be tied to the public Whipping post and Receive twenty five Lashes on his bare back well laid on between the hours of three and five O'clock this afternoon.

David Worley and David Mahon proved that they attended five days each as witnesses for the State agst. Margaret Richey including milage.

Ordered that Court be adjourned till tomorrow morning ten O'clock

Thursday morning August 21st day 1788 The Court met according to adjournment present the same Judges as before.

(p 292) The Atto. for the State enters A Noli prosiqui upon the Indictment against John Sevier and Thomas Conway.

JOHN DENN on the Demise)plt.)
of WILLIAM SHARPE   )   (
         against   (In Ejectment.
RICHARD FENN ----------deft)
                    This day came the plt. by his Atto. and it appearing by the affidavit of George Rutledge that Henry Kalbock Tennant in possession of the premises hath been duly served with a Copy of the plts. declaration and of the note there under written and the said Henry Calbock not appearing nor any person claiming Title to the premises.
It is Considered by the Court that the plt. recover against the said deft. his Term yet to come of and in the lands & appurtenances in the declaration mentioned & a writ of Habere facias possessionint awarded to put him in possession thereof.

The Grand Jury came into Court and presented an Indictment against John Sevier Junier and Thomas Conway Endorsed "A True bill" and also an Indictment against John Gaywood Senr John Pemberton, Daniel Lambert, Robert Gowan, Jesse Vaughter, Francis Berry, Philemon Vaughter, William Delany, Stephen Majors, John Laughlin Senr. John Sharp, Edward Sterling, John Gossarch and Jacob Bealor, Endorsed a true bill upon which Indictment, without Capias Francis Berry and Jesse Vaughter, appeared at the Bar were charged and upon hearing the charge plead not guilty and for tryal hereof put themselves upon the County at the next Term.

Francis Berry personally appeared in Court and acknowledged himself indebted to the people of this State in the Sum of One Hundred Pounds, to be levied of his goods and chattels lands and Tenements Yet upon this Condition that he do appear at the next Court to be holden for this District to answer what shall then and there be objected against him and James Stuart acknowledges himself indebted to the people of this State in the Sum of Fifty pounds to be levied as above with this Condition (p 293) that the Said Francis Berry do appear as he hath bound himself to do.
Jesse Vaughter Principal personally appears in Court and acknowledges himself indebted to the people of this State the Sum of One Hundred pounds and James Stuart and Dillen Blevins his Securities also personally appear and acknowledge themselves indebted to the people of this State in the Sum of Fifty pounds each to be levied of their goods and Chattels lands tenements respectively. But to be void on condition that Jesse Vaughter appear at the next

Court to be holden for this District and there answer the Charge of the
State, exhibited against him and abide by the Judgment of the said Court.

(p 294) At a Superior Court of Law began and held for the District of
Washington at the Court house in Jonesboro the Sixteenth day of February
Anno Domine 1789.

Present the Honorable:
        David Campbell, Esquire Judge.

Proclamation was made for all Justices of the peace Sheriffs, Coroners
and other Officers, that have taken any Inquisitions or recognizances,
whereby you ____ let any person to bail, or have any process to return put
in your records thereof forthwith, that the peoples Judges may proceed
thereon.
Whereupon Michael Harrison Esquire Sheriff of the County of Washington
made return upon the Venire Facias to him directed for that County that he
had Summoned Lanton Carter, Andrew Greer, John Campbell, John Strain, John
Wear, Abednigo Inman, John Hammer, Henry Nelson, James Montgomery Moses
Carson, John Alexander, David Carson, William Cobb, Joseph Greer and Thomas
Rogers.
and John Hunt Esquire Sheriff of Hawkins County Returned upon the venire fa-
cias to him directed for said County that he had Summoned Arthur Galbraith,
David Hamlin and Joseph McMinn.
And William McCormack Esquire Sheriff of Sullivan County returned up the
Venire facias to him directed for that County that he had Summoned William
Delaney Alexander Laughlin, Thomas Elliot, Samuel Smith, David Looney, Will-
iam Nash, John Anderson, Peter Morrison, Daniel Perry, John Scott, William
McCormack and John Blevins.
And James Richardson Esquire Sheriff of Greene County returned upon the
venire facias to him directed for that County that he had Summoned John New-
man, David Russell, John Stone, Robert McCall, William Morrow, Joseph Gist,
Henry Conway, David Kerr, Alexander Outlaw, and Shadrach Morriss.
                              es
Out of which venire facias*the following persons was Elected, impannelled,
A Foreman appointed and a Jury sworn to enquire and presentment make for the
body of this District on behalf of the State, To wit, (p 295) Andrew Greer
Foreman James Montgomery, John Campbell, John Wear, John Stone, William Nash
David Russell, Joseph Gist, Henry Nelson, William Morrow, William McCormack,
David Carson, William Delaney, Arthur Galbraith, Samuel Smith, Alexander Out-
law, David Kerr, and Alexander Laughlin and with drew from the bar to consid-
er of their presentments.

Ordered that Noah Hawthorn a Constable attend upon the grand Jury, who was
accordingly Qualified for that purpose .

Ordered that the Court be adjourned till tomorrow morning nine O'clock.

Tuesday morning the 17th of February 1789.
    The Court met according to adjournment.

THE STATE OF NORTH CAROLINA) plt)
  against   (Upon an Indictment for an Assault
JOHN CAYWOOD & Others (Defts) and Battery

        Plea of Defendants Not Guilty. This day
came the Attorney for the state, and the defendants by their Attorney,
and thereupon came also a Jury to wit John Hanner Moses Carson, Thomas
Rogers, Daniel Hanlin, Joseph McMinn, Peter Morrisson, John Scott, John
Alexander and Henry Conway who being elected tried and sworn the truth to
speak upon the Issues Joined upon their Oaths do say that the Defendants
John Caywood Senr. John Penberton, Daniel Lambert, Robert Cowan, Jesse
Vaughter, Francis Berry, Philemon Vaughter, William Delaney, Stephen Majors
John Laughlin, John Sharpe Edmund Sterling, Jacob Boalor and John Goascorch
are not guilty of the Tresspasses assault and Battery Charged against them
in the bill of Indictment.

(p 296) On Motion of Waightstill Avery Esqr. Atto. for James Edens praying
a writ of Error against John Tipton Executor and Susannah Pugh Executrix of
the estate of Jonathan Pugh deceased (administrators of Simon Bundy) for
reasons shewn to this Honble Court, Ordered therefore that a writ of Error
Issue for the Causes and reasons set forth in the Complainant and that a
summons Issue to the Sheriff of Washington Commanding him to Summon the said
John Tipton and Susannah Pugh Exr. as aforesaid to appear on the Fifteenth
day of August next and answer James Eden as aforesaid of his said Writ of error to reverse the Judgment of the County Court of Washington as set forth
in his Complaint.
Reasons for Error filed with the other papers of this Suit.

Ordered that the Court be adjourned till tomorrow morning nine O'clock.

Wednesday morning February the 20th day 1789.
The Court met according to adjournment.

EDMUND WILLIAMS --------plt.) upon an appeal from a Judgment of
  against   (County Court of Washington Obtained
JOHN ABDIR and WILLIAM MOORE Dfts.) by the plaintiff against the Defendants
 (Adair)   This day came the parties by their Attor-
         neys, and thereupon came also a Jury to
wit John Hanner, Moses Carson, Thomas Rogers, Daniel Hanlin, Joseph McMinn,
John Scott, John Newman, Robert McCall, John Strain, John Alexander, Abednigo
Inman and David Looney who being elected tried, and sworn the truth to speak
upon the Issue Joined upon their Oath do say that the defendants are guilty
in manner and form as the plaintiff against them hath complained, and they
do assess the plaintiffs damages by Occasion thereof to One Hundred and sixty nine pounds twelve shillings besides his Costs, therefore it is considered by the Court that the Said plaintiff recover against the said defendants
his (p 297) damages aforesaid in form aforesaid assessed and his Costs by
him about this suit in this behalf expended and the said defendants in mercy.

STATE of NORTH CAROLINA---pltff.)
  against   (Upon an Indictment for an Assault & Battery.
RUSSELL BEAN--------------Deft)

The defendant Russell Bean Saith that he is not guilty in manner and form as in the Indictment against him is alledged and of this he puts himself upon the County, and the attorney who for the people of the State in this behalf prosecutes in like manner, and thereupon Came a Jury to wit. Joseph Ford, Moses Carson, Thomas Rogers, Daniel Hamlin, Joseph McMinn, John Scott John Newman, Robert McCall, John Strain, John Alexander, Abednigo Inman and David Looney who being elected tryed and Sworn the truth to speak upon the Issue Joined upon their Oaths do say that the defendant Russell Bean is guilty of the trespass assault and Battery in manner and form as in the Indictment against him is alledged. Therefore it is Considered by the Court that the aforesaid Russell Bean be taken to satisfy the people of this State of his fine by Occasion of the trespass, assault and Battery aforesaid _____

On motion of Waightstill Avery Esqr. Attorney William Cocke praying a mendamus to admit the said William Cocke to the office of Clerk of the Court of pleas and Quarter Sessions for the County of Washington ____ Ordered that the same be admitted to record - the further Consideration of which is now post poned.

Nathaniel Henderson Esqr. Coroner for Hawkins County makes return of the Following inquisition by him Taken which is in the words following towit,

STATE OF NORTH CAROLINE) Issd.
HAWKINS COUNTY   )
                    Inquisition
indented, Taken (p 298) at the dwelling House of John Waddle in the County aforesaid, on the 5th day of September 1788 upon the view of the body of Joseph Erwin late of the County aforesaid then and there lying dedd and upon the oath of John King, William Armstrong Arthur Galbraith, Samuel McPheters John Waddel, Thomas Taylor, James Hamilton, Nathaniel Watson, James Cooper, Lambert Layne, Thomas King and Robert Cooper, who being sworn and charged to enquire when where how and in what manner the said Joseph Erwin came to his death do say upon their Oath that the said Joseph Erwin came by his death by the fire of a Pistol accidentally In the Hand of Luces Widener, and that from the testimony and other circumstances the death of the said Erwins was by no means intended by the Said Widener and that it was altogether an accident. Given under our Hands and Seals this 5th day of September 1788.
John King (Seal)   Wm Armstrong (Seal)
Arthur Galbraith (Seal)   Saml. McPheters (Seal)
John Waddel   (Seal)   Thomas Taylor   (Seal)
James Hamilton   (Seal)   Nathan Watson   (Seal)
James Cooper   (Seal)   Lambert Layne   (Seal)
Thomas King   (Seal)   Robert Cooper   (Seal)

NATHANIEL HENDERSON Cor. (Seal)

EDMOND WILLIAMS ----------------plt.)
        against   (
JOHN ADDIR and WILLIAM MOORE- Defts)
    (Adair)   Waightstill Avery Esqr. Attorney for

the defendant moves that the Judgment in this Case be arrested. It is considered by the Court that the above motion be over ruled

Ordered that the Court be adjourned till tomorrow morning nine Oclock -

Thursday morning February the 19th day & 1789

Court met according to adjournment.

(p 299)　STATE OF NORTH CAROLINE)plt)
　　　　　　against　　　　　　　　　(Upon an Indictment for a petit Lar
　JOHN COLYER ------------Deft) cenys being an appeal from the Judg-
　　　　　　　　　　　　　　　　　　　ment of the County Court of Washington ____

　　　　The Defendant John Colyer Saith he is not guilty in manner and form as in the Indictment against him is alledged and of this he puts himself up-in the Country. and the Attorney who for the people of this State in this behalf prosecutes in like manner and thereupon Came a Jury to wit, John Strain John Hammer, John Alexander, William Cobb, Thomas Rogers, Daniel Hamlin Moses Carson, John Scott, Robert McCall, Shadrach Morriss, David Looney, and Abednigo Inman, who being elected tried and Sworn the truth to speak upon the Issue Joined upon their oaths do say that the Defendant John Colyer is not guilty of the Petit Larceny as Charged against him in the bill of Indictment.

Ordered that the Court be adjourned till to morrow Morning ten O'clock.

Friday Morning February the 20th day 1790 ? (1789)
Court met according to adjournment.

STATE OF NORTH CAROLINE --plt)
　　　　against　　　　　　　　(The fine of the Defend and Russell Bean is
RUSSELL BEAN ------------Deft) assessed by the Court at twenty five pounds
　　　　　　　　　　　　　　　　　good and Lawfull Money of the State aforesaid
to the use and behoof of the people of the Said State and it is further ad-judged by the Court here that the said Russell Bean remain in close Jail un-till he make his said fine to the people of this State together with the Costs of this Suit.

WILLIAM COX ----------appellee) Upon an appeal from a Judgment of the County
　　　　vs　　　　　　　　　　(Court of Washington obtained (p 300) by
BENJAMIN COBB----------appellant) the Appellee against the appellant.
　　　　　　　　　　　　　　　　　This day came the appellant by his Attorney
and thereupon came also a Jury to wit, John Strain, Abednigo Inman, John Ham-mer, Moses Carson, John Alexander David Looney, Thomas Rogers, Daniel Hamlin, Joseph McMinn, John Scott, John Newman, and Shadrach Morris, who being elect-ed and Sworn the truth to speak upon the Issue Joined and the appellee being Called but failing to appear, It is therefore Ordered that he be non suit and that the appellant recover against the appellee his costs by him in this be-half expended and the said appellee in Mercy.

ALEXANDER MOFFITT------plt.)
　　　　against　　　　　　(Case, Defamitory Words.
ROBERT IRVINE -------Dft.) Pled Justification.

This day came the parties by their Attornies and thereupon came also a Jury towit, the Same Jury that were on the last Suit who being elected tried and Sworn the truth to Speak upon their Oaths do say that that is guilty in manner and form as the plaintiff against him hath Complained and they do assess the plaintiffs damage by Reason thereof to fifty Pounds besides his Costs.

Therefore it is Considered by the Court that the plaintiff recover against the Defendant his damages aforesaid in form aforesaid assessed and his Costs by him about his Suit in this behalf expended, and the said Defendant is in Mercy.

Ordered that the Court be adjourned till tomorrow morning ten Oclock.

Saturday Morning February 21st day 1789.
Court met according to Adjournment.

Ordered that Edmond Williams Esquire Sheriff of Washington County be Amerced in the Sum of Twenty pounds payable to the people of the State of North Carolina, for having failed to Return Two Original, (p 301) processes (towit) Thomas Stripling against Alexander Moffit, and Others. and Clayton Stripling against the same unless Satisfactory Cause and Reasons Shall be here after Shewn to the Court why the above processes were not returned.

STATE OF NORTH CAROLINA ----plt.)
      against   (Upon an Indictment for an Assault an_ Riot.
JAMES KUYKINDOLL----------Dft.)

                      The defendant James Kuykindoll being Charged upon this bill of Indictment and asked Concerning the different facts therein alledged against him for answer saith that he is not guilty of them or any of them in manner and form as against him in the Indictment is alledged and of this he puts himself on the Country. And the Attorney who for the people of this State on this behalf prosecutes in like manner therefore thereupon Comes a Jury (towit) Moses Carson John Strain, Abednigo Inman, John Alexander, John Hammer, David Looney, Thomas Rogers, William Cobb, Joseph McMinn, John Scott, John Newman and Shadrach Morriss who being elected tried and Sworn the truth to speak upon the Issue Joined upon their Oaths do say that the defendant James Kuykendoll is not guilty in manner and form as in the Indictment against him is alledged whereupon it is Conjectured by the Court that the Said Defendant be discharged, upon paying the Costs of this Suit.

ANDREW GREER ------------plt.)
      against   (In an action of Replevin on a case agreed.
EDMOND WILLIAMS Sheriff-Dft)

                      The Court here having heard the alligations of the said parties and already understood the merits of the above Case by them agreed and having duly attended to the several acts of assembly in that case made and provided.

It is therefore Considered by the Court that the said Edmond Williams Esqr. the afore mentioned high Sheriff (p 302) of Washington County is not justifyed by the laws of the land for having Seized and destroyed the property of the Said Andrew Greer for the levying a tax of eighteen Shillings to wit,Nine Shillings in Current money and nine Shillings in Certificate &c. for each of

the three polls for which the said Andrew Greer was accountable, But the
Tax of Twelve Shillings to wit Six Shillings Current money and Six Shillings
Certificates &c. on each of the Said Polls tendered to the Said Sheriff by
the Said Andrew Greer as the only legal tax which the said Sheriff ought to
have levyed on the Said Andrew Greer for the said three polls for the year
aforesaid the Said Tax of twelve Shillings for the year aforesaid. in current
money and certificates &c. On each poll in the District of Washington being
equal to the Tax on three Hundred acres of Land in the said District according to the act of the general assembly in that case made and provided.
It being the opinion of the Court here that the poll Tax in the District of
Washington, (It being on the west Side of the Appalachian Mountains) is no
more to be regulated by the Tax on lands on the East Side of those Mountains
than the poll tax on the inhabitants on the East Side of the Said Mountains
is to be regulated by the tax on lands in the said district of Washington on
the west Side of the Said Mountains. And that the said Horse so destrained
by the said Sheriff be returned and restored to the said Andrew Greer he the
said Andrew Greer paying and discharging to the said Sheriff the Tax of twelve
Shillings that is to say Six Shillings in Current Money and Six Shillings in
Certificates &c. on each of the aforesaid three polls and that the said Sheriff do pay the costs of this action of Replevin.

Waightstill Avery Esquire attorney for William Cocke withdraws the motion
that he made to this Court for a mandamus to Issue to the Court of Washington
County.

(p 303) Ordered that the Clerk of this Court receive the fees pointed out in
the fee bill before the resolution in all Casses that is not since provided
for and there being no law since directing any fee upon indictments to the
Clerks of the Superior Courts; It is Considered by the Court that the old law
allow six shillings and eight pence upon Indictments is still in force in the
State as well since as before the revolution.

Ata Superior Court of Law begun and held for the District of Washington at
the Court House in Jonesboro the Fifteenth day of August Anno Domini 1789
and Fifteenth of American Independence.

Present the Honorable
                        David Campbell esqr. Judge.

Proclamation was made for all Justices of the peace, Sheriff Coroners, and
other officers; that had taken any Inquisitions, or recognizances where by
any person had been let to bail, or that had any other process to return to
put in their records thereof; that the States Judges might prosecute thereon.

Whereupon Michael Harrison esquire Sheriff for County of Washington returned
upon the Venire Facias to him directed for that County that he had Summoned
Landon Carter, John Tipton, James Stuart, William Cox, Andrew Greer, William
Stephenson, James Montgomery, Joseph Tipton, John Hammer, Joseph Greer, Robert
Love, John Blair, David Carson, John Milligan and William Trimble, also James
Richardson esquire Sheriff for the County of Greene returned upon the Venire
Facias to him directed for that County that he had Summoned Joseph Harden Senr.

James Lea, Adam Dunwoody, Joseph Conway, Benjamin Gist, John Newman, John Gordon, Henry Earnest; William Shadrach Inman, John Gass, Major Temple, James Mahan, James Hill, Alexander Outlaw, Robert Allen, Robert Campbell, Daniel Kennedy, Samuel Dunwoody Benjamin Gest, (p 304) John McNabb and David Russell.

Also William McCormack esquire Sheriff for the County of Sullivan returned upon the Venire facias to him directed for that County, that he had Summoned David Perry, James McNair John Pemberton, William Evans, John Laughlin, John Vance, Timothy Acoff, David Looney, Thomas Titsworth, John Duncan, John Gaywood Senr. and Abraham McClelland.

Likewise John Hunt esquire Sheriff for the County of Hawkins returned upon the Venire Facias to him directed for that County that he had Summoned Samuel Wilson, Nathaniel Austin and Thomas Berry - Out of which several Venire Faciases the following persons were elected impannelled and Sworn as a grand Jury of inquest to enquire for the State and the body of this District (towit) Daniel Kenneday Foreman Samuel Wilson, Samuel Dunwoody, Joseph Gass, Major Temple, William Stevenson, Robert Campbell, Joseph Conway, Robert Love, William Evans, John Milligan, David Perry, David Russell John Vance, Robert Allen, John Pemberton, Henry Earnest and John Hammer received their charge and withdrew from the bar to enquire of their presentments

Ordered that the Court be adjourned till Monday Morning ten Oclock.

Monday Morning August 21st day 1789.
  Court met according to adjournment.

ALEXANDER BAINE ---plt.)
    against   (being a Suit brot. for the recovery of a debt
JOHN KING ------Deft.) upon a bond.

                    The Defendant pleads the General Issue payment and
Set off.
        This day came the parties by their attornies and thereupon came
also a (p 305)   Jury (towit) John Tipton; William Cox, James Montgomery, Joseph Greer, John Blair, John Newman, Shadrach Inman, James Hill, James Lea, Adam Dunwoody, Benjamin Gist and David Carson who being elected tried and Sworn the truth to Speak upon the Issue Joined upon their Oath do say that the Defendant John King did make the writing Obligatory (as mentioned in the plaintiffs declaration) for the Value of Fifty nine pounds Nineteen Shillings and Eight pence Current Money of the common wealth of Virginia equal in value to Sixty Six pounds and Seven pence farthing and the Jurors aforesaid assess the damages of the said Alexander Baine on that Occasion to Sixty Six pounds and Seven pence farthing current Money of this State and the expenses and Costs by him laid out in the prosecution of this Suit.
      Therefore it is Considered by the Court that the said Alexander Baine recover against the Said John King his said Debt and damages of Sixty six pounds and Seven pence farthing assessed by the Jury together with the Costs of this Suit - and the Said John King is in Mercy.

GEORGE MITCHELL---plt.)
    against   (An Action on the Case for defamitory words spoke
WILLIAM COX------Deft.) by the Defendant of the plaintiff - upon the hear-
                                        ing of the plaintiffs declaration the Defendant by
his Attorney pleads General Issue with Leave -----Upon which Issue came
the parties this day by their attorneys and thereupon Came also a Jury (towit) Landon Carter, Andrew Greer, Timothy Acoff, John Laughlin, Thomas Titsworth, John Duncan, Abram McClelland, Nathaniel Austin, Thomas Berry, John
Gordon, John McNabb and James McNair, who were elected, tried and Sworn the
truth to speak upon the Issue Joined, Upon their Oath do say that the Defendant William Cox is guilty in manner and form as the plaintiff against him
hath Complained and they (the (p 306) Jury aforesaid) do assess the plaintiffs damages by Occasion thereof to Two pounds and Six pence besides his
Costs. Therefore it is Considered by the Court that the Said plaintiff recover against the said defendant his damages aforesaid in form aforesaid assessed and his Costs by him about this Suit in this behalf expended and the
Said William Cox is in mercy &c.

On motion of Waightstill Avery Esqr. attorney for Christian Rhodes. Ordered
that in the Suit of William Wharton against the Said Christian Rhodes a notice to the Attorney at law for the said William Wharton for the Cross examination of the defendants Witnesses shall be deemed Sufficient; the said William Wharton not residing within this district and not having any know agent
in the Same.

STATE OF NORTH CAROLINE ---plt.)
    against   (Upon an Indictment for Robbery.
JOHN SEVIER Junr.----------Deft.)
                            Ordered that this Indictment be Quashed and
the defendant discharged.

Ordered that Court be adjourned till tomorrow morning nine O'clock.

Tuesday the 13th day of August 1789.
    Court met according to adjournment.

Upon Sufficient reasons which have been shown and made known to the Court
by Edmond Williams esqr. late Sheriff of the County of Washington it is Ordered that he be released from the payment of the Sun where in he was Amerced at the last term.

On affidavit of Joseph Greer (filed) Ordered that the Clerk of Washington
County Issue letters of Administration on the Estate of Edmund Carter deceased who died intestate, and take Security in the Sun of one (p 307) thous-
and pound with two free holders and that he be qualified as administrator.

BENJAMIN COBB-----------plt.)
    against   (Upon an appeal from a Judgment of the County
EDWARD CALAHAN----------Dft.) Court of Washington.

This day came the parties by their Attornies and thereupon Came also a Jury

towit Landon Carter, John Tipton William Cox, Andrew Greer, James Montgomery, John Blair, Daniel Carson, Adam Dunwoody, Benjamin Gist, John Newman, Shadrach Inman, and James Hill whowere elected try'd and sworn the truth to speak upon the Issue Joined do say upon their Oath that the find specially for the plaintiff and assess his damage to eight pounds for the Costs mentioned in the Declaration besides his Costs upon this promise - If the testimony of Mary Chote should be considered valid in Law which we the Jury aforesaid refer to the Court and if the testimony of Mary Chote should by the Court be adjudged not valid we find for the Defendant. ____
Upon argument of the above Special verdict The Testimony of the aforesaid Mary Chote is adjudged by the Court to be valid and good - Therefore it is considered by the Court here that the aforesaid Benjamin Cobb the plaintiff recover against the said Edward Callahan the Defendant his damages aforesaid in form aforesaid assessed and his Costs by him about his suit in this behalf expended and the Said defendant is in Mercy &c.

```
SAMUEL HARRISS----------plt.)
         against              ( In Ejectment
CHRISTIAN SHULTZ-----Deft.)
```

This day came the parties by their Attorneys and thereupon came also a Jury (towit) John Laughlin, Timothy Acoff, Thomas Titsworth, John Duncan, John Caywood, Abram McClelland, Thomas Berry, John Gordon, John McNabb, Alexander Out- (308) law, James Lea and Joseph Greer, who being elected tried and Sworn the truth to Speak upon the Issue Joine'd do say upon their Oath do say that the defendant Christian Shultz is guilty in manner and form as the plaintiff against him hath declared, and that they do assess the plaintiffs damages by Occasion thereof to Six pence besides his Costs Therefore it is Considered by the Court that the plaintiff recover against the Defendant his term yet to Come, of and in the Lands and tenements with the appurtenances in the declaration mentioned Together with Six pence damages and his Costs by him about his Suit in this behalf expended @ and the said defendant may be taken ____

Ordered that the Court be Adjourned till tomorrow morning nine O'clock___

Wednesday Morning the 19th day of August 1789.
Court met according to adjournment.

```
JOHN DENN on the demise )        )
of JOHN SHELBY-----------)plt (
         against                 ( Injectment
RICHARD FEN--------------Deft.)
```

John Arranwine on his motion is admitted defendant in this Suit in the room of the said Richard Fen and thereupon by William Cooke Esqr. his Attorney he comes and defends the force and inquiry when and pleads the general Issue Confesses the lease entry and Ouster in the declaration supposed and agrees to insist on the title only at the trial, Whereupon this day Came the parties by their Attorneys and thereupon came also a Jury (towit) William Cox, James Hill, John Newman, Abram McClelland, James Montgomery, Nathaniel Austin, Adam Dunwoody, John Blair, Landon Carter, David Carson, James Lea, and Thomas Titsworth who being elected try'd and Sworn the truth to speak upon the Issue Join'd do say upon their Oaths that the defendant John Arranwine is guilty in manner and form as the plaintiff against him hath declared and that they do assess the plaintiffs damages by occasion thereof to six pence, (p 309) besides his Costs. Therefore it is considered by the Court that the plaintiff recover against the defend- and his term yet to come, of and in the Lands and Tenements with the Appur- tenances, in the declaration mentioned together with Six pence damages, and his Costs by him about his Suit in this behalf expended and the said defend- ant be in Mercy &c.

David Looney being summoned to appear at this Court a witness in the above Suit being Solemnly Called, failed to appear it was thereupon Ordered that he be fined agreeable to act of assembly, and that a Scire facias Issue to Noti- fy him to appear at next term and shew Cause if any he can why execution ag- ainst his goods &c. Should not Issue.

```
JOHN DEN on the demise)plt )
of SAMUEL HARRISS      (      ( In Ejectment
          against       (
RICHARD FENN-----------Deft)
```

Charles Hayes upon his motion is admitted defend- ant in the room of Richard Fenn and thereupon by Waightstill Avery Esqr. his attorney comes and defends the force and injury &c and pleads the General Is- sue, Confesses the Lease, entry and Ouster in the declaration Supposed and to insist upon his title only at the trial, whereupon this day came the par- ties by their attornies, and thereupon came also a Jury (towit) John Tipton, Andrew Greer, Joseph Greer, Benjamin Gist, Shadrach Inman, John Laughlin, Timothy Acoff, John Duncan, John Caywood, Thomas Berry, John Gordon & John McNabb who being elected try'd and sworn the truth to speak upon the Issue join'd upon their Oath do say That the Defendant Charles Hayes is Guilty in manner and form as the plaintiff against him hath declared and that they do assess his damages to Six pence besides his Cost, therefore it is considered by the Court, That the plaintiff recover against the Defendant his term yet to come of and in the lands & (p 310) tenements with the appertenances in the declaration mentioned together with Six pence damages and his Costs by him about his Suit in this behalf expended and the said Defendant be in Mercy.

```
ARTHUR COBB---------plt)
      against          ) Debt in the nature of a Covenant.
VALENTINE SEVIER-Deft )
```

This day came the parties by their Attorneys, and thereupon came also a Jury (towit) Landon Carter, William Cox, James Mont- gomery, John Blair, David Carson, James Lea, Adam Dunwoody James Hill, Alex- ander Outlaw, James McNair, Abram McClelland and Thomas Titsworth who being elected tried and sworn the truth to speak on the Issue joined upon their Oath do say That the obligation mentioned in the plaintiffs declaration is the deed of the defendant and assess the plaintiffs damage for the non per- formance of the Condition thereof to one Hundred and three pounds besides his Costs therefore it is Considered by the Court Here that the plaintiff recover against the Defendant his damages aforesaid in form aforesaid asses- sed and his Costs by him about his Suit in this behalf expended and the said defendant is in Mercy.

ABEL WESTFALL ----------plt.)
    against   (Trover.
GEORGE GILLISPIE-----Deft.)

                       The defendant by his Atto. Saith he is not Guilty in manner & form as the plaintiff hath Set forth in his declaration and of this he put himself upon the County. Whereupon this day Came the parties by their Attornies and thereupon Came also a Jury (towit) John Tipton, Andrew Greer, Joseph Greer, Benjamin Gist, Shadrach Inman, John Laughlin, Timothy Acoff, John Duncan, John Keywood, Thomas Berry, John Gordon and John McNabb, Who being elected, tried, and sworn the truth to speak upon the Issue Joined upon their Oath do say, they find (p 311) the Defendant guilty of the trover and conversion set forth against him in the plaintiffs declaration and they assess his damage by reason thereof to Forty pounds besides his Costs, Therefore it is considered by the Court here that the plaintiff recover against the Defendant his damages aforesaid in form aforesaid assessed, and his Costs by him about his suit in this behalf expended, and the Said Defendant is in Mercy.

JOHN DENN on the demise of)plt)
MARK MITCHELL-------------)   (
     against   ) <u>injectment</u>
RICHARD FEN--------------Deft)

                       Samuel Smith upon his motion At February term Last past was admitted Defendant in the room of the aforesaid Richard Fenn and thereupon by his Attorney James Rease Esqr. he Comes and defends the force and injury, and pleads the General Issue confesses Leave, Entry and Ouster in the declaration Supposed and agrees to insist upon the Title only at the trial, Whereupon this day came the parties by their attornies and thereupon came also a Jury (towit) Landon Carter, William Cox, James Montgomery, John Blair, David Carson, James Lea, Adam Dunwoody, James Hill, Alexander Outlaw, James McNair, Abram McClelland, and Thomas Titsworth, and being elected and tried, and Sworn, the truth to Speak upon the Issue Joined upon their Oath do say, that the Defendant Samuel Smith is Guilty of the Trespass in ejectment in manner and form as the plaintiff against him hath declared and that they do assess his damage by Occasion thereof to Six pence besides his Costs, Therefore it is considered by the Court here, that the plaintiff Mark Mitchell recover against the Defendant Samuel Smith his term yet to come of and in the Lands and Tenements with the appurtances in the Declaration mentioned, together with Six pence damages, and his Costs by him in this behalf expended and said Defendant is in mercy.

(p 312) Court adjourned till to Morrow morning 9 O'clock.
Thursday Morning 20th of August __ Court met according to adjournment.

William Pemberton Son of John Pemberton being Solemnly Called upon to appear and give evidence in the Suit of Armstead Blevins against John Caywood as he by Subpoena was bound to do, and he failing to appear, It is ordered by Court that he be fined Conditionally agreeable to act of assembly, and that Scire Facias Issue for him to appear at next Term to Shew Cause if any he can why execution against his Estate Should not Issue.

PATRICK SHIELDS------plaintiff) an Action on the case for Defamitory words
       against   (spoken of the plaintiff by the Defendant.
NICHOLAS MESSER----Defendant)

                  Upon the Hearing of the plaintiffs declarations
the Defendant by his attorney Comes and defends the wrong and for plea Saith
That he is not guilty of Speaking the words charged in the declaration, and of
this he puts himself on Country, and the plaintiff doth the like also, Where-
upon by the Court here a Jury to be Impannelled was awarded them whereupon
Came the parties by their Attorneys and thereupon came also the following
Jury (towit) John Tipton, Andrew Greer Joseph Greer, Benjamin Gist, Shadrach
Inman, John Laughlin, Timothy Acoff, John Duncan, John Keywood, Thomas Berry
John Gordon and John McNabb who being elected, tried and sworn, the truth to
Speak upon the Issue Joined upon their Oath do say that the Defendant is guil
ty in manner as alledged against him by the plaintiff and assess his damages
by reason thereof to Forty Shillings and Six pence. Therefore it is Considered by the Court here that the plaintiff recover against the Defendant his
damages aforesaid in form aforesaid, assessed and his Costs by him about his
suit in this behalf expended and the said Defendant is in Mercy.

(p 313)   JOHN DENN on the demise   )
          of ANDREW ENGLISH ------plaintiff (
               against   (In Ejectment
          RICHARD FENN-----------Defendant)

                  George Martin upon his Motion
is admitted Defendant in the room of Richard Fenn and by William Cooke Esqr.
his attorney Comes and defends the force and injury &c. and pleads the General Issue Confesses Lease, entry and Ouster in the declaration Supposed and
agrees to insist upon the titles only at the trial, whereupon this day Came
the parties by their Attorneys and thereupon Came also a Jury (towit)
Landon Carter, William Cox, James Montgomery, John Blair, David Carson, James
Lea, Adam Dunwoody James Hill, Alexander Outlaw, James McNair, Abram McClell-
and and Thomas Titsworth, who being elected, tried and Sworn the truth to
speak upon the Issue joined upon their Oath do say That they find the Defendant guilty of the trespass in ejectment in manner and form as the plaintiff
against him hath declared, and that they do assess his damage by reason there
of to Six pence besides his Cost. Therefore it is considered by the Court
here That the plaintiff recover against the Defendant his term yet to come
of and in the lands and Tenements with all the Appurtenences in the declarati
on mentioned together with Six pence damages and his Costs by him about his
Suit on that behalf expended, and the said Defendant be in Mercy.

Ordered that Court be adjourned till tomorrow Morning Nine O'clock.
Friday Morning 21st of August 1789.
Court met according to adjournment.

STATE OF NORTH CAROLINA-- plaintiff) Indicted for
         against   (horse Stealing.
DANIEL COLLUM------------Defendant)

                Whereupon the Defendant was charged and
asked concerning the facts alledged against him in the indictment for answer
(p 314) Saith he is not Guilty as the bill of indictment against him is alledged and of this he puts himself upon the Country. And the attorney who

for the people of this State prosecutes in like manner, Thereupon Came
a Jury (towit) John Tipton, William Cox, James Montgomery, David Carson,
John Newman, Adam Dunwoody, Shadrach Inman, James Hill, John Laughlin,
Thomas Titsworth, John Duncan and John Keywood who being elected tried and
Sworn, the truth to speak upon the Issue Join'd - upon their Oath do say
"the the Defendant is not guilty in manner and form as charged in the bill
of Indictment, Whereupon it is considered by the Court that he be discharged upon his paying the costs of this Suit, for which he may be taken.

THE STATE OF NORTH CAROLINA ----plaintiff)
           against   (Indicted for
DAVID STUART----------------------Defendant)

                            The Defendant being charged upon
his bill of Indictment and asked concerning the facts therein alledged against him Saith That he is guilty of the   whereof he stands indicted whereupon it is considered by the Court here that the Defendant David Stuart be
amerced in the Sum of Ten pounds good and Lawfull money of the State aforesaid to the use and behoof of the people of the said State. Together with
the Costs of this Suit, for which he may be taken.

STATE OF NORTH CAROLINA-----plaintiff)
           against   (Indicted for Raising men to oppose the
JOHN HOWARD--------------------Defendant) Collection of publick Taxes & for op-
                                      posing the Collection

The Defendant John Howard being Charged upon the bill of Indictment and asked concerning the different facts therein alledged against him for answer
Saith that he is not guilty of them or any of then in Manner and form as
against him is set forth in the bill of Indictment and of this he puts him-
self upon the County and William Cocke Esquire who for - (p 315) the people of this State prosecutes puts it upon the Country in like manner.
Whereupon a Jury to try &c was awarded then (towit)
John Tipton, James Montgomery, John Newman, James Lea, Adam Dunwoody, James
Hill, John Laughlin, Thomas Titsworth, John Duncan, John Keywood, Abram Mc-
Clelland, and Nathaiel Austin, who being elected tried and Sworn the truth
to Speak upon the Issue Joined upon their oath do say, That the Defendant
John Howard is not guilty of the first Charge alledged against him of Raising men; But that he is guilty of the Second Charge (towit) of opposing the
collection of the public Taxes, whereupon it is considered by the Court that
the said John Howard be amerced the Sum of Ten pounds Current Money to the
use and behoof of the people of this State. Together with the Costs of this
suit for which he may be taken.

STATE OF NORTH CAROLINA - plaintiff)
           against   (upon an Indictment for an assault and
BENJAMIN MCCUSTON-------- Defendant)   Battery.

                            The Defendant being charged upon the bill
of Indictment and asked concerning the facts exhibited against him Saith that
he is guilty of the Trespass assault & Battery wherewith he stands Charged.

Whereupon it is considered by the Court here that the Defendant Benjamin McCuston be amerced the sum of five pounds current Money to the use and behoof of the people of this State; together with the Costs of this Suit for which he may be taken.

STATE of NORTH CAROLINA- plaintiff)
        against   (upon an Indictment for an Assault &
WILLIAM SMALL-----------Defendant)   Battery

                           The Defendant pleads Guilty, and by the Court is fined Twenty Shillings and the Costs of this Suit. For which he may be taken.

(p 316) STATE of NORTH CAROLINA - plaintiff)
              against   (Upon an Indictment for a petit
      DAVID LARKINS------------Defendant)Larceny in the County Court of
                                      Hawkins
                           This being an appeal from the said Court. The Defendant upon being charged in the County Court and asked Concerning the premises to which he replyed that he was not guilty and for this he put himself upon the Country, Whereupon in this Court a Jury was awarded them (towit) John Tipton, James Montgomery John Newnan, Samuel Lea, Adam Dunwoody James Hill, John Laughlin, Thomas Titsworth, John Duncan, John Keywood, Abram McClelland and Andrew Greer, who being elected tried and sworn to speak upon the Issue Joined upon their Oath do say, That the Defendant is not guilty in manner and form as set forth in the bill of Indictment. Therefore it is considered by the Court here that the said David Larkins be forthwith discharged upon his paying the Costs of this Suit, for which Costs he may be taken.

STATE OF NORTH CAROLINA - plaintiff)
      against   (Upon an Indictment for Horse Stealing
EDWARD JERVIS-------------Defendant)
                         The Defendant Edward Jervis being charged upon the bill of Indictment, and asked Concerning the facts alledged against him in said bill saith he is not guilty in manner and form as set forth in the bill and of this he puts himself upon the Country and the Attorney who prosecutes on behalf of the State doth the Same also. Whereupon Came the same Jury that was upon the last Cause, who being elected tried and Sworn the truth to speak upon the Issue Joined upon their oath do say that the Defendant is not guilty of the Felony & Horse Stealing in manner & form as against him is alledged. Therefore it is considered by the Court here that the said Edward Jervis be forthwith discharged, upon his paying the Costs of this suit.

(p 317) STATE of NORTH CAROLINA- plaintiff)
              against   (
      DAVID DEADERICK----------Defendant)The Defendant being Indicted for
                          having committed a trespass assault & Battery and being charged upon the bill of Indictment and asked what he had to say concerning the Said Trespass Saith that he is guilty thereof in manner and form as set forth against him, Whereupon it is considered by the

Court here that the said David Deaderick be amerced the sum of Forty Shillings Current money to the use & behoof of the people of the Said State together with the Cost of this Suit, for which he may be taken.

JAMES EDEN-----------------------------plaintiff)
      against   (
JOHN TIPTON and SUSANNAH PUGH   ) Upon a writ of Error to Reverse
administrators on the Estate   (a Judgment of the County Court
of JONATHAN PUGH who was adminis-) of Washington
trator of SIMON BUNDIES ESTATE   )

                            The Court having heard the Errors assigned, and Clearly understood the same together with the allegations of the Parties Thereon; Therefore have considered that the Judgment of the County Court of Washington (obtained by Jonathan Pugh administrator against James Eden) for the Errors assigned as aforesaid and others appearing in the records, and proceedings thereof, be vacated, reversed, Therefore nothing had, and that the said John Tipton, and Susannah Pugh pay the costs on this behalf expended for which they are in mercy.

Ordered that Court be adjourned untill Tomorrow Morning Nine O'clock.

Saturday Morning 22nd of August 1789.
Court met according to adjournment.

on motion made and affidavit filed by George Mitchell Ordered that a Mandamus in the alternative Issue to the County Court of Washington to allow the Said George Mitchel his appeal at the Suit of John Carney.

(1790)

(p 318) At a Superior Court of Law begun and held for the District of Washington at the Court house in Jonesboro the Fifteenth day of February Anno Domini 1790 and in the   year of American Independence.

Present the Honorable David Campbell Esquire Judge; who in Pursuance of an act of the Congress of the United States entitled "An act to regulate the time and manner of administering certain Oaths Took the oath to Support the Constitution of the United States.

Francis A. Ramsey Clerk of this Court also took the aforesaid Oath.

Michael Harrison Esquire Sheriff of the County of Washington, James Richardson Sheriff of the County of Greene, William McCormack Esquire Sheriff of the County of Sullivan and John Hunt Esquire Sheriff of the County of Hawkins all appeared in open Court and took the Oath to Support the Constitution of the United States.

Proclamation was made for all Justices of the peace Sheriffs, Coroners and other officers, that had taken any Inquisitions, or recognizances, whereby any person had been let to bail, or that had any other processes to return forthwith to put in their records thereof that the States Judges might proceed thereon, as by law directed. Whereupon James Richardson Esquire Sheriff of

the County of Greene made return that he had executed the writ of Venire
Facias to him directed upon the following persons (towit) Joseph Harden,
John Newman, David Russell, Robert Campbell, George Pearce, John Blackbourne
Joshua Gist, George Doherty, William Nelson, Peter Fine, Elisha Baker, John
Murphy, Francis Hughes, Charles Robison, Asahal Rawlings, Richard Woods,
Laughtr Armstrong and David Rankin. And William McCormack Esquire Sheriff
of the County of Sullivan that he had executed the Writ of Venire Facias
to him directed upon the following persons (towit) upon George Vincent Rich-
ard Gammon, John Caywood Senr., Robert Easley, Daniel Wright, John Miller,
Richard Murr, Michael (p 319) Craft, William Scott, Andrew Crocket, John
Yancey and John Pemberton.
And John Hunt Esquire Sheriff of the County of Hawkens makes return of the
Writ Venire Facias to him directed that he had executed the Same upon William Armstrong Senr. William Armstrong Junr. and Richard Grantham. and Mich-
ael Harrison Esquire Sheriff of the County of Washington Returns that he had
executed the Writ Venire Facias to him directed for the Said County upon the
following persons (towit) upon James Stuart, William Purselly, Joseph Brittain
James Carmichael, William Nelson, Henry Nelson, Landon Carter, John Hammer,
James McCord, John Campbell Esqr. Abednigo Inman, John Tipton, John Strain,
Andrew Duncan, and John Campbell Captain. From the before mentioned Venire
Faciases were elected the following persons for a grand inquest, to enquire
for the people of this State and the body of this District to wit, James
Stuart(who by the Court is appointed Foreman) Robert Easly, Richard Gammon,
Richard Grantham, James McCord, William Purselly, Joseph Brittain, John New-
man, Michael Craft, Abednigo Inman, David Ranken, William Scott, John Miller,
William Armstrong Junr., John Pemberton, Lanty Armstrong, Robert Campbell and
Francis Hughes, who being Sworn, were Charged and withdrew from the Bar to
consider of their presentments.

Peter McNamee is appointed a Constable to attend upon the Grand Jury and
was Sworn accordingly.

Orderedthat the Court be adjourned untill tomorrow Morning nine Oclock

Tuesday morning 16th of February
                Court met according to adjournment.

DAVID LARKINS-----------plaintiff)
                against   (Upon an appeal from a Judgment of the
CORNELIUS RAYGAN---------Defendant) County Court of Hawkens.

Upon (p 320) a Suit Brot.there by the said David against the Said Cornelius for having Slandered and defamed his Character and the Said Cornelius
after having heard the plaintiffs declaration by William Sharpe Esquire his
attorney comes and defends the injury and what ever else he ought to defend
and for plea Saith that he is not guilty of Slandering the plaintiffs Character in the form and manner that he against him hath alledged, and further
pleads Justification as to part of the Charges and of this he puts himself
upon the Country, and the plaintiff by his attorney doth the Same. Whereup
on this day came the parties by their Attornies and thereupon Came also a
Jury (towit) Joseph Harden,David Russell, George Pearce, Joshua Gist,William

Nelson, Peter Fine, Elijah Baker, Charles Robison, Asahel Rawlings,Richard
Wood, George Vincent, and John Caywood, who being Elected tried and sworn the
truth to Speak upon the Issue Joined upon their Oath do say, that the_ find
for the plaintiff and assess his damage to Fifty Shillings besides his Costs,
Therefore it is Considered by the Court here that the Said plaintiff David
Larkens recover against the said Defendant Cornelius Raygan his said damages
in form aforesaid assessed to Fifty shillings and his Costs by him about this
Said Suit on that behalf expended and the said Defendant in mercy.

JOHN DENN on the demise of JOHN LOYD- plaintiff)
        against   (a declaration in Ejectment
RICHARD FENN--------------------------- Defendant)

James Jervis on his motion is admitted defendant in the room of Richard Fen
and by his Attorney comes into Court and Confesses, Lease, Entry and Ouster,
and for plea Saith he is not guilty agrees to insist only upon his Title at
the trial and of this he puts himself upon the Country, which doth the plaintiff also, Therefore hereupon Came the parties by their attorneys and thereupon Came also a Jury (towit) David Wright, Richard Murrell, Andrew Crocket,
John Yancy, William (p 321) Armstrong Senr. James Carmichael, Henry Nelson,
William Nelson, John Hammer, John Campbell Esqr., John Tipton and Andrew Duncan, who being elected tried and Sworn the truth to Speak upon the Issue
Joined upon their Oath do say, that the_ find the Defendant guilty of the
Trespass in Ejectment, as the plaintiff against him hath declared, and that
they assess his damage by reason thereof to six pence besides his Costs by
him in this behalf expended. Therefore it is Considered by the Court, That
the plaintiff recover against the Defendant his term yet to come of and in
the lands and Tenements with the appurtenances in the declaration mentioned
together with six pence damage and his Costs by him about his Suit on that
behalf expended and the said Defendant in Mercy.

ISAAC BULLER----plaintiff) Being an action on the Case for the Recovery of
        vs   (a Negro paid for by the plaintiff to the Defend-
JOHN TADLOCK----Defendant) ant.

                    The Defendant hearing the plaintiff declaration
Comes and defends the injury and wrong done and for plea Saith that he is
not guilty in manner and form as the plaintiff against him hath alledged
and of this he puts himself upon the Country as doth the plaintiff also,
Whereupon this day Came the parties by their Attornies and thereupon Came also
a Jury (towit) Joseph Harden, David Russell, George Pearce, Joshua Gist,
William Nelson, Peter Fine, Elijah Baker, Charles Robison, Asahel Rawlings
Richard Wood, George Vincent and John Caywood, who were elected Tried and
Sworn the truth to speak upon the Issue Joined upon their oath do say, That
they find the Defendant Guilty, as the plaintiff against him hath alledged
and assess his damage by reason thereof to One hundred pounds besides his
Costs by him on this behalf expended. Therefore it is Considered by the
Court here that the said Isaac Buller recover against the said John Tadlock
his damages aforesaid in form aforesaid assessed to One Hundred pounds and
(p 322) Also his Costs by him expended in the prosecution of this his said
Suit and the Said John Tadlock in Mercy.

On Complaint of Michael Looney Guardian of Henry Sampson Larkens.
Ordered that a Certiorari Issue to the Justices of Hawkens County, commanding them to certify all the proceedings had and done before them Relative to the appointment of Guardians to the Said Henry Sampson Larkens an Orphan and the management of his Estate.

Ordered that Court be adjourned untill tomorrow Morning nine of the Clock.

Wednesday Morning 17th of February. Court met according to adjournment

STATE of NORTH CAROLINA---plaintiff)
    against   (Upon a Indictment for a Trespass assault
WILLIAM BELL--------------Defendant) and Battery.

        The Defendant being Charged upon the bill
of Indictment and asked concerning the facts alledged against him in the Said
Bill Saith that he is not guilty of any of them and of this he puts himself
upon the Country which doth the attorney who prosecutes for the Government
also whereupon Comes the Same Jury that was sworn upon the Issue between
Isaac Bullar and John Tadlock who being elected tried and sworn the truth to
say upon the Issue Join'd upon their Oath do say, That the Defendant is Guilty in manner & form as Charged in the bill of Indictment and as the Attorney
for the State in his Replication hath alledged. Therefore it is Considered
by the Court, That the Defendant William Bell be amerced the sum of Fifteen
pounds Current Money to the Use and behoof of the people of this State, and
that he remain in Close Custody untill he make his Fine to the people of this
State, Together with the Costs expended in this prosecution for which the
Defendant be taken.

(p 323) STATE of NORTH CAROLINA---plaintiff) Upon an appeell from the
     against   (County Court of Greene upon a
   DANIEL HILL--------------Defendant) Judgment of the said Court up
                on an Indictment for a Trespass in which Richard Brindlee
prosecuted on behalf of the State.
        The Defendant having been Charged upon the said bill and
asked concerning the Several facts therein alledged against him for plea Saith
that he is not guilty and of this he puts himself upon the Country and the
Attorney who behalf of the State prosecuted does the same also, upon which
Issue of Traverse a Jury is Awarded them (towit) David Wright, Richard Murrell, Andrew Crocket, John Yancy, William Armstrong, James Carmichael, William
Nelson, Henry Nelson, John Hammer, John Campbell, John Tipton, and Andrew Duncan, who were elected, tried and Sworn the truth to Speak upon this Issue of
Traverse upon their Oath do Say, That the defendant Daniel Hill is not guilty
of the trespass in manner and form as charged in the bill of Indictment.
Therefore it is Considered by the Court that the Said Daniel Hill be forthwith
discharged and it is further considered and adjudged by the Court that the
aforesaid Richard Brindlee the prosecution for his false clamour, and Malicious prosecution of this Suit pay the Costs that have been expended thereon for
which he the said Richard Brindlee be taken.

STATE of NORTH CAROLINA--plaintiff)
      against   (Upon an Indictment for Horse Stealing.
BENJAMIN GOODIN-----------Defendant)

                    The defendant being arraigned and charged
upon the bill of indictment, and asked whether he was Guilty of the Felony
and Horse Stealing Charged against him therein to which he plead he was not
guilty and of this he put himself upon the Country and William Cocke Esqr
attorney to prosecute on behalf of the State doth the same, whereupon this
day came a Jury (towit) Joseph (p 324) Harden, David Russell, George Pearce
and Joshua Gist, William Nelson, Peter Fine, Elisha Baker, Charles Robison,
Asahel Rawlings, Richard Wood, George Vincent and John Caywood, who were
elected tried and sworn, the truth to speak upon the Issue Join'd upon their
oath do say that the Defendant Benjamin Gooden is not Guilty of the Felony
and Horse Stealing whereof he stands Charged in the bill of Indictment Therefore it is considered by the Court that the said Benjamin Gooden be forthwith
discharged upon his paying the Costs of this prosecution for which he may be
taken.

BENJAMIN HARDEN-----plaintiff)
      against   (Case
JAMES PICKENS------Defendant)

                    After hearing the plaintiffs declaration the
Defendant by James Reese Esqr. his attorney Comes Defends &c and for plea
Saith that he is not guilty as the plaintiff against him hath alledged and
has leave to give Special matter in evidence and of these he puts himself
upon the Country, and the Attorney for the plaintiff doth likewise, Whereupon this day came the parties by their Attornies and thereupon Came a Jury
(towit) David Wright, Richard Murrell, Andrew Crocket, John Yancy, William
Nelson, Elisha Baker, Charles Robison, James Carmichael, William Neilson,
Henry Nelson, John Hammer and John Campbell who were elected tried and sworn
the truth to speak upon the Issue Joined upon their Oath do say, That the
find for the plaintiff and assess his damage to Forty five pounds Thirteen
Shillings besides his costs by him in this Suit expended, Therefore it is
considered by the Court here That the said Benjamin Harden recover against
the said James Pickens the aforesaid Sum of Forty five pounds Thirteen Shillings together with the Costs by him expended in the prosecution of this Suit,
and said Defendant in mercy.

(p 325) Ordered that Court be adjourned untill tomorrow Morning nine O'clock.

Thursday Morning 18th of February

Court met according to adjournment.

STATE of NORTH CAROLINA-----plaintiff)
      against   (Upon an indictment for Horse Stealing.
JOHN WILSON--------------------Defendant)

                    The Defendant John Wilson being arraigned
and Charged upon the bill of Indictment and asked concerning the charges exhib
ited against him therein Saith that he is not guilty and of this he puts himself

upon the Country and William Cocke Esquire who prosecutes as attorney on behalf of the State, doth the Same Whereupon this day came a Jury (towit) Peter Fine, Charles Robison, William Nelson, Andrew Crocket, Robert Rogers, Nathaniel Davis, James Pickens, Andrew Belfor, John Young, Joseph McCorkle, George Mitchell, and John King, who were elected tried and Sworn the truth to Speak upon the Issue Joined upon their Oath do say, That the Defendant John Wilson is Guilty of the Felony and horse Stealing in manner and form as the Attorney for the State in his replication hath alledged and as charged in the bill of Indictment. The Sentence of the Court is post poned.

Ordered that Court be adjourned till to morrow Morning Nine of the Clock.

Friday Morning 19th of February,
    Court met according to adjournment.

ELIZABETH LOONEY----------plaintiff)
        against   (Upon a Complaint for Slander.
AGNESS GRAY ------------- Defendant)
                                Referred by the parties to George Maxwell, William Cage and William Nash who returned into the Court the following award (towit) we George Maxwell, William Cage and William Nash to whom was referred (p 326) the determination of the above Suit after hearing the allegations of the parties and attended and attended duly to their evidences do award the Defendants pay the Costs of this Suit, Signed by the above named arbitrators.
Therefore it is considered by the Court that the Defendant Agness Gray pay the Costs expended in the prosecution of this Suit .

STATE of NORTH CAROLINA---plaintiff)
        against   (Indicted for assault.
JOSEPH HARDEN--------------Defendant)
                                Upon being charged upon the bill of Indictment and asked concerning the facts Exhibited against him Says he is guilty of the Charges brot against him. Whereupon it is considered by the Court that the Said Joseph Harden be amerced in the sum of Forty Shillings Current money to the use and behoof of the people of this State together with the Costs of this Suit for which he may be taken.

JOHN DEn on the demise of)plaintiff)
MARY MITCHELL----------- ((
        against   (In Ejectment
RICHARD FEN--------------Defendant)
                                Jason Cloud upon his motion is admitted Defendant in the room of Richard Fenn and by William Sharpe Esquire his Attorney comes and defends the force and injury and what ever else he ought to defend and for plea Saith he is not guilty and confesses Lease, entry, and Ouster, and agrees to insist upon his Title only at the trial and for this puts himself upon the Country and John McNairy Esquire for the plaintiff doth the Same also, whereupon the following jury is awarded them (towit) Richard Murrel, John Yancy, Andrew Crockett, Elisha Baker, David Wright, James Carmichael, George Vincent, George Pearce, John Caywood, Peter Fine, William Nelson of Greene, and William Nelson of Washington who were elected

tried and Sworn the truth to speak upon the Issue Joined upon their Oath do say, That the find the Defendant Jason Cloud Guilty of the (B 327) Trespass in Ejectment in manner and form as charged in the declaration, and assess the plaintiffs damages by reason thereof to Six pence besides his Cost by him on this behalf expended.

Therefore it is considered by the Court here that the plaintiff recover against the said Defendant, his Term yet unexpired of and in the Lands and Tenements, with the appurtenances in the declaration mentioned together with six pence damages, and his Costs by him about his Suit in this behalf expended for which he may have a Writ of Fieri Facias and Helieri Facias Possessionim, and the Said Defendant in Mercy.

Ordered that Court be adjourned till tomorrow morning Nine of the Clock.

Saturday Morning 20th of February
Court met according to adjournment

STATE ofNORTH CAROLINA -----plaintiff) Upon an Indictment for Horse Stealing
    against (
JAMES FULSOM----------------Defendant)

The Defendant be arraigned and charged upon the bill of Indictment and being asked if he was guilty of the Felony and horse Stealing therein exhibited against him? for answer saith he is not guilty; and of this he puts himself upon the Country; and William Cocke Esqr. who on behalf of the State prosecutes likewise Thereupon a Jury is awarded (towit) John Campbell, Captain John Hammer, William Armstrong,Landon Carter, John Tipton, David Russell, Henry Nelson, Richard Woods, Joshua Gist Asahel Rawlings, Charles Robison and John Campbell Esquire who were elected tried and sworn the truth to speak upon the Issues Joined upon their Oath do say, That the Defendant James Fulson is Guilty of the Felony and Horse Stealing in manner and form as charged in the bill of Indictment.
The Sentence is post poned.

(p328) STATE of NORTH CAROLINA--plaintiff)
     against (Upon an appeal from the County
    SAMUEL BEARD---------------Defendant) Court of Greene.

It appearing from the papers which are produced and the Transcript of the record in this Suit That the Defendant Submitted to Court, Thereupon Virtually Confessed himself guilty of the alledged against him. It is therefore the opinion of this Court, that the Judgment of the County Court aforesaid, in fixing the prosecution with the Costs; be reversed and wholly set aside, and it is Judgment of this Court that the Defendant Samuel Beard be amerced in the sum of Forty Shillings to the use and behoof of the people of this State, together with the payment of the Costs of this Suit, for which he may be taken.

Orderedthat Court be adjourned untill Monday Morning Ten O'clock.

Monday morning Twenty Second of February.
  Court met according to adjournment.

STATE OF NORTH CAROLINA)
    against   (
JOHN WILSON and   (Who by the Jury are found Guilty of Horse
JAMES FULSON   )   Stealing.

                  Being called to the bar and asked what they had to
say why Sentence agreeable to Law Should not be passed upon them Say nothing. It is therefore Ordered that the said John Wilson and James Fulson
be confined in the publick pillory for the Space of one Hour that each of
them have both their Ears nailed to the pillory, and Severed from their
heads. That they receive at the publick whipping post Thirty nine Lashes
upon their bare backs, well laid on, and that each of them be Branded upon
their right Cheek with the letter H. and on their left cheek with the letter T and that the Sheriff of Washington County put this Sentence into execution between the Hours of Twelve and four this afternoon.

(p 329) Michael Harrison Esquire Sheriff of Washington County being one
of the officers of this Court and Solemnly Called upon and failing to appear. It is therefore ordered that for his said failure he be amerced in
the sum of two pounds to the use and behoof of the people of this State.

JAMES CARMICHAEL-----plaintiff)
    against   (Being an action for Debt Brot. by the plain
JOHN WILSON and   )Defendants(tiff against the said Defendants in the
JOHN TATE   )   (County Court of Greene from the Judgment
                      of which an appeal was Granted, and it appears from the Transcript of the Record that came from the Court below that
the Defendants had plead the General Issue and set off, and the parties
Join Issue upon that plea whereupon this day came the parties by their Attornies and thereupon Came also a Jury (towit) John Campbell Esquire, John
Tipton, John Campbell Captain, John Hammer, Henry Nelson, William Nelson,
William Armstrong Senr. John Yancy, Andrew Crockett, Richard Murrell, David
Wright and John Caywood, who were elected tried and Sworn the truth to speak
upon the Issue Joined upon their oath do say, That the find for the plaintiff
and assess the Value of his Debt and Interest to Sixty five pounds and two
pence Fathering- besides the Costs of this Suit.
Therefore it is considered by the Court here that the said James Carmichael
Recover against the said John Wilson and John Tate or either of them the sum
of Sixty five pounds and two pence farthing his debt aforesaid in form aforesaid assessed Together with the Costs expended in the prosecution of this
Suit. And the said Defendants in mercy.

WILLIAM DOLPHIN, a Black man---plaintiff)
    against   (The plaintiff Declaration charges the
JOHN TADLOCK-------------------Defendant)Defendant with a Trespass vias armis
                      and False Imprisonment.
                      Being a Suit Brot. by the plaintiff
for the recovery of his Freedom, The Defendant by William Cocke Esquire his
Attor- (p 330) ney Defends the force injury and whatever else he ought to
defend, and for plea saith he is not guilty and prays for leave to give the
special matter on Evidence and of this he puts himself upon the Country and

Waightsell Avery Esquire Attorney for the plaintiff doth the Same also, Whereupon came the following Jury (towit) Joseph Harden David Russell, George Pearce, Joshua Gist, Peter Fine, Elisha Baker, Charles Robison Asahel Rawlings, Richard Wood, George Vincent, John Campbell and James Carmichael who were elected, tried and sworn the truth to speak upon the Issue Join'd upon their Oath do say, That the_ find the Defendant Guilty in manner and form as charged in the plaintiffs declaration and assess his damage by Reason thereof to One Shilling and the Costs of this Suit. Therefore it is considered by the Court that the said William Dolphin is a free man, recover against the said John Tadlock his damages aforesaid in form aforesaid assessed to one Shilling Current money and also the Costs by him Expended in the prosecution of this his Said Suit and the Said Defendant in Mercy.

Ordered that Court adjourned untill tomorrow Morning Nine O'clock.

Tuesday Morning 23rd of February
    Court met according to adjournment.

STATE OF NORTH CAROLINA---plaintiff)
            against   (Indicted for a misdemeanor in Office
JOSEPH HARDEN Senior-------Defendant)as a Justice of the peace.

                        The Defendant being Charged Upon the bill of indictment and asked if he was guilty of the misdemeanor therein alledged against him, answers that he is not guilty thereof and of this he puts himself upon the Country, and William Cocke Esquire who was attorney for the State prosecutes doth the Same Whereupon the following Jury was awarded (towit) William Nelson, William Armstrong, John Yancy, John Campbell Captain, Andrew Crockett, Peter Fine, David Wright, John Campbell Esquire, John Caywood, (p 331) George Pearce, Henry Nelson and George Vincent who were elected, tried and sworn the truth to Speak upon the Issue Join'd upon their Oath do say, That the Defendant is not guilty in manner and form as charged in the Bill of Indictment. Therefore it is Considered by the Court that the said Joseph Harden be forthwith discharged, upon his paying the Costs of this Prosecution for which he may be taken.

STATE OF NORTH CAROLINA-------plaintiff)
        against   )   (Indicted for a misdemeanor in con-
JOSEPH WILSON   )   ) cealing of a Creature known by
SAMUEL WILSON   (Defendants   (them to be Stolen.
WILLIAM WILSON &((
WILLIAM BUCKNER)   )

                        The Defendants being Charged upon the bill of Indictment and Severally asked if they were Guilty of the Misdemeanor therein alledged against them. Say that they are not Guilty and of this they put themselves upon the Country and William Cocke Esquire Attorney for the State doth the same Whereupon the following Jury was awarded them (towit) Peter Fine, Elisha Baker, Charles Robison, John Caywood, Richard Murrell Andrew Crocket, John Yancy, William Nelson, Henry Nelson, John Hanner, John Campbell, Esquire, and John Campbell Captain who were elected, tried and Sworn the truth to speak upon the Issue Join'd upon their Oath do say that the Defendants Joseph Wilson Samuel Wilson, William Wilson and William Buckner Guilty of the Misdemeanor in manner and form as charged in the Bill of Indictment - Therefore it is Considered by the Court that the said Joseph Wilson, Samuel Wilson, William Wilson, and William Buckner Stand each of them One Hour in the pillory Be amerced in the Sum of Ten pounds Each to the use and behoof of the people of this State and to pay the Costs of this prosecution and to be imprisoned untill the said Fine or amercement and Costs be paid for which they may be taken.

(p 332) Ordered that Court be adjourned untill tomorrow Morning Nine O'clock

Wednesday Morning 24th February
            Court met according to adjournment.

JOHN STONE-plaintiff))
      against   (theplaintiffs declares in Case. The Defendants plee
RICHARD WOOD-Defendant)the General Issue.

            This day came the parties by their Attornies and there upon came also a Jury (towit) William Nelson, William Armstrong, John Yancy, John Campbell Cap., Andrew Crocket, David Wright, John Campbell Esqr. John Caywood, Henry Nelson, George Vincent, John Tipton, Richard Murrell, who were elected tried and sworn the truth to speak upon the Issue Join'd upon their oath do say That the Defendant is Guilty in manner and form as set forth in the plaintiffs declaration, and do assess his damage by reason thereof to six pence besides his Costs by him expended, about the prosecution of this suit.
Whereupon William Sharpe Esquire attorney for the Defendant moves for a New Trial and for reasons appearing to the Court, Ordered that the Same be Granted and this suit continued Untill next Term.

(p 333) At A Superior Court of Law begun and held for the District of Washington at the Court House in Jonesboro the Sixteenth day of August Anno Domini 1790 and in the 15th year of American Independence.

Present the Honorable David Campbell Esquire Judge.

Proclamation was made for all justices of the peace Sheriff, Coroner, and other officers, That had taken any inquisitions, or recognizances; whereby any person had been let to bail or that had any other process to return, Forthwith to put in their records thereof that the States Judge may proceed thereupon as by Law is directed.
            Whereupon James Richardson Esquire, Sheriff of Greene County returned that he had executed the Writ of Venire Facias to him directed upon the following persons (towit) Joseph Harden Senr., John Newman, David Russell, Ashael Rawlings, John Cass, John Stone, James Hill, Michael Rawlings, Peter Blake, George Pearce, Robert Campbell, Alexander Outlaw, Richard Woods, Joseph Conway, Joseph Harden Junr., Jesse Hoskens, William Horner, William Conway, Major Temple, Henry Conway, James Lea, and William Morrow.
            Whereupon also George Rutledge EsquireSheriff of the County of Sullivan Returned that he had executed the writ of Venire Facias to him directed

upon the following persons (towit) John Caywood Senr. William McCormack, David Bragg, John Duncan, Samuel Brashiers, James Campbell, David Perry, Joseph Rhea, Christopher Acoff, William Hughes, Alexander McClelland and David Wright.

Whereupon Thomas Berry Esquire, Sheriff of the County of Hawkins also Returns that he had executed the Writ Venire Facias to him directed upon the following persons (towit)
Arthur Galbraith, William Armstrong, and Thomas Gibbons. (p 334) And Michael Harrison Esquire, Sheriff of the County of Washington Returns that he has executed the Writ Venire Facias to him directed upon the following persons (towit) Joseph Brittain John Hammer, Joseph Crouch, Zachariah McCubbin, Benjamin Holland, John Tipton Senr. Garrett Reasoner, Abednigo Inman, John Strain, John Kerr Senr. Pharoah Cobb and Alexander Moffit.

From the above mentioned Venire Facias, The following persons were elected to serve as a Grand Jury to Enquire for the people of this State; and the body of this District at this Term (towit) John Tipton who by the Court is appointed Foreman, Henry Conway, David Brag, John Duncan, John Newman, Joseph Rhea, William Morrow, Joseph Harden, Senr. Alexander Moffit David Russell , John Caywood Senr., AlexanderOutlaw, Zachariah McCubbin John Gass, Richard Wood, Jessee Hoskins, Joseph Brittain, and Peter Blake who being Sworn were charged, and withdrew from the Court to Consider of their presentments.

Ordered that William McCloud be appointed Constable to wait upon the Grand Jury who came into Court and was Qualified accordingly

Ordered that Court be adjourned untill tomorrow morning Nine of the Clock.

    Tuesday morning 17th of August,
        Court met according to adjournment.

ARMSTEAD BLEVINS by next Friend -plaintiff)
        against   (An action Brot. for Defamitory
JOHN GORSORCH-------------------Defendant) words spoken by the Defendant
                                           of the plaintiff.

The Defendant by William Sharpe Esquire his attorney Comes and defends the Injury and wrong done, and Saith that he is not guilty of speaking the false Slanderous words Charged in the plaintiffs declaration and prays for leave to give the special matter in evidence and pleads also the Statute of Limitations and of all these (p 335) he prays to be enquired by the Country, and Waightstill Avery Esquire Attorney for the plaintiff doth the same also, Whereupon came the following Jury (towit) John Hammer, George Pearce, Mayor Temple, Robert Campbell, James Hill, John Strain, James Lea, Benjamin Holland, Abram McClelland, Thomas Gibbons, Arthur Galbraith and Joseph Crouch, who being elected, tried and sworn the truth to speak upon the Issue Joined, upon their Oath do Say That the_ find the Defendant guilty of Speaking the Defamitory words as the plaintiff against him in his declaration hath alledged, and assess his damage by reason thereof to Forty Shillings and Costs by him expended in the prosecution of this Suit, Therefore it is considered by the Court; That the Said Armstead Blevins, Recovered his said damages against the said John Gorsorch in form aforesaid assessed to Forty Shillings Together with his Costs about his Suit on this behalf exped. and the said Defendant in mercy.

A Bill of Sale from Landon Carter to George Mitchell for a negro Boy named Claybourne was proved in open Court by the oath of William Cocke a Subscribing Witness Thereto and the Same is ordered to be registered.

DAVID ALLISON ------plaintiff) Being an action Brot by the plaintiff
   against   (against the Defendant for Detaining a negro
GEORGE MITCHELL-----Defendant) Boy named Claybourne which the plaintiff
                              claims as his property.
                          The Defendant by William Cocke Esquire his
attorney comes and defends the Injury and Wrong complained of by the plaintiff and for plea Saith he does not detain the plaintiffs property and of this he puts himself upon the Country and the Attorney for the plaintiff doth the same also. Whereupon this day came the plaintiffs by their Attorneys and thereupon came also a Jury (towit) William Hughes, James Campbell David Perry, David Wright, William Horner, William Conway, Michael Rawlings Andrew Greer, Joseph Conway, William McCormack, Samuel Brashier, and William Armstrong who were elected tried and Sworn (p 336) The truth to speak upon the Issue John'd upon their oath do say, That the Defendant George Mitchell does detain the negro Claimed in the Declaration which they Value to Two Hundred and Fifty pounds upon which William Cocke Esquire attorney for the Defendant moves for a new trial in this Suit and for reasons appearing to the Court, Ordered that the same be granted.

Ordered that Court be adjourned untill tomorrow morning Nine of the Clock.

Wednesday Morning 18th of August.
    Court met according to adjournment.

JOHN COLYER-----plaintiff)
    against   (An action Brot. for Defamitory words spoken of
RICHARD PIG-----Defendant) the plaintiff by the Defendant.
                          The Plaintiff being solemnly Called to appear
and prosecute his said Suit, It is therefore ordered that he be non suited and pay the Costs of this Prosecution.

HEZEKIAH BALCH administrator)   ) Debt
of the Estate of   (plaintiff) and
HANAH LEWES Deceased   )   (
    against   ) Deniet
BENJAMIN LEWES -------------- Defendant)
                          The Defendant by William Sharpe Esquire his attorney Defends the force &c and pleads non Detinct with leave to give the special matter in Evidence and pray it be put upon the Country and the plaintiff Likewise.
    Whereupon this day came the parties by their attornies and thereupon came also a Jury (towit) John Hammer George Pearce, Major Temple, Robert Campbell James Hill, James Lea, Benjamin Holland, Abraham McClelland, Thomas Gibbons,

Arthur Galbraith, Joseph Crouch and William Hughes, who were elected, tried and Sworn the truth to speak upon the Issue Joined upon their oath do say, That the find for the plaintiff and assess his damage to ThreeHundred and Thirty Three pounds Thirteen Shillings and four pence with Lawfull interest from the time that the Bond mentioned in the plaintiffs declaration (p 337) became due together with his Costs by him expended on this behalf - The plaintiff Releases Thirty Eight pounds Eleven Shillings and four pence part of the Interest upon the said verdict which Leaves Three Hundred and Ninety five pounds

It is therefore Considered by the Court that the above named Hezekiah Balch as administrator of the Estate of Hannah Lewes Deceased do recover of the Defendant Benjamin Lewes his damages aforesaid in form aforesaid assessed to Three Hundred and Ninety five pounds Together with the Costs by him expended in the prosecution of this suit, and the Defendant in mercy.

```
JAMES ALLISON --------plaintiff)
          against               (
EZEKIEL ABELL )                 )
NATHAN DAVIS  (                 (  Trespass &c.
JOHN FERGUSON )       Defendants)
& THOMAS TIPTON)                )
```

The Defendants by John McNairy Esquire their Attorney Comes and defends the Trespass and Wrong complained of and pleads the General Issue and Statute of Limitations and put themselves upon the Country and Waightstill Avery Esquire Attorney for the plaintiff doth the same, Whereupon this day came the parties by their Attorneys and thereupon came also a Jury (towit) James Campbell, David Perry, Abednigo Inman, David Wright, William Horner, William Conway, Michael Rawlings, Andrew Greer, William McCormack, Samuel Brashiers, William Armstrong, and John Kerr who were elected tried and sworn the truth to speak upon the Issue Joined upon their Oath do say, That the find the Defendants not Guilty in manner and form as charged in the plaintiffs declaration, Therefore it is considered by the Court that the said James Allison plaintiff pay unto the said Defendants the Costs by them on this behalf expended, and for his false Clamour he may be taken.

```
(p 338)  JAMES ALLISON - plaintiff ) An action on the Case for a Trespass
              against               ( of assault and Battery by the Defendant
         NATHAN DAVIS ---Defendant ) upon the plaintiff for which he sues &c
                                     Upon hearing the plaintiffs declaration
```
The Defendant by John McNairy Esquire his attorney Comes and defends the force & Injury and for plea Saith that he is not guilty, Justification and the Statute of Limitations and of these he puts himself upon the Country, and Waightstill Avery Esquire attorney for the plaintiff doth the same also, whereupon the following Jury was awarded them (towit) George Pearce, Mayor Temple Robert Campbell, James Hill, Benjamin Holland, Thomas Gibbons, Arthur Galbreath, Joseph Crouch Joseph Harden, Christopher Acoff, and John Stone who were elected, tried and Sworn the truth to speak upon the Issue Joined upon their oath do say, That the find the Defendant is not Guilty of the Trespass assault and Batter in manner and form as charged in the plaintiffs declaration, Therefore it is considered by the Court that the Defendant be forthwith

discharged and that the plaintiff pay unto him his Costs by him on this behalf expended, for which he may be taken.

CLAYTON STRIPLING ---plaintiff)
       against   (The Plaintiff by William Cocke Esqr his
ALEXANDER MOFFIT)   ) Attorney complains of the Defendants &c
JOHN TIPTON Junr. (Defendants) in custody &c for a Trespass Assault and
ANDREW CALDWELL)   (Battery, and False Imprisonment.
JOB ODELL and   (   )
ADAM RADER   )   ) The Defendant upon hearing the declaration
                                By Waightstill Avery Esquire their Attor-

ney Comes and defends the force injury and wrong and pleads the General Issue and Justification and of this put themselves upon the Country, and William Cocke attorney for the plaintiff doth the same Likewise Whereupon the following Jury was awarded them (towit) William Armstrong James Lea, Abram McClelland, William Hughes, James Campbell, David Perry, Abednigo Inman, David Wright, (p 339) William Horner, William Conway, Michael Rawlings and Andrew Greer who were elected tried and Sworn the truth to speak upon the Issue Joined, upon their Oath do say, That the Defendants are not Guilty in manner and form as Charged in the plaintiffs declaration, Therefore it is considered by the Court that the Defendants be forthwith discharged and that they recover against the plaintiff their Costs and charges by them in this behalf expended for which he may be taken.

Ordered that Court be adjourned untill tomorrow Morning nine of the Clock.

Thursday morning 19th of August.

Court met according to adjournment.

STATE of NORTH CAROLINA ----plaintiff)
        against   (Upon a Indictment for Horse Stealing
ELIAS PY COWINE ----------Defendant)

                              The Defendant being arraigned and charged upon the bill of Indictment, and asked whether he was Guilty of the Felony and Horse Stealing charged against him in the bill of Indictment, To which he answers he is not Guilty and of this he puts himself upon the Country and William Cocke Esquire attorney on behalf of the State doth the same likewise whereupon the following Jury was awarded them (towit) John Strain Major Temple, Arthur Galbraith, William Conway, Landon Carter, James Lea, Benjamin Holland, James Campbell, James Hill, John Kerr, William McCormack, and Michael Rawlings, who were lected tried and sworn the truth to speak upon the Issue Join'd upon their Oath do say That the Defendant Elias Py Cowrne is Guilty of the Felony and Horse Stealing whereof he stands Indicted in manner and form as charged In the Bill of Indictment, Sentence by the Court is postponed untill a further day.

(p 340)   STATE OF NORTH CAROLINA---plaintiff)
                against   (Indicted for a Trespass.
            ALEXANDER GOODEN----------Defendant)
                                  The Defendant being Charged

upon the bill of Indictment and asked whether he was Guilty of the Trespass alledged against him saith that he is not Guilty and of this he puts himself upon the Country and William Cocke Esquire who on this behalf prosecutes on behalf of the State doth the same likewise. Whereupon a Jury was awarded then (towit) John Hanner George Pearce, Robert Campbell, James Hill, Major Temple, John Strain, Thomas Gibbons, Arthur Galbraith, Benjamin Holland, Joseph Crouch, William Hughs, and David Wright, who were elected tried and sworn the truth to speak upon the Issue Join'd upon their oath do say That the Defendant is Guilty in manner and form as Charged in the bill of Indictment. Therefore it is considered by the Court that the said Alexander Gooden, be amerced in the sum of Ten pounds Current Money, to the use and behoof of the people of This State; and that he pay the Costs expended in the prosecution of this Suit, for which he may be taken.

STATE OF NORTH CAROLINA ----plaintiff)
       against   (Indicted for a Trespass.
JAMES GOODEN---------------------Defendant)

                     The Defendant being Charged upon the bill of Indictment and asked whether he was guilty of the Trespass alledged against him, Saith that he is not guilty; and of this he puts himself upon the Country, and William Cocke Esquire Attorney for the State doth the Same also, whereupon came a Jury (towit) James Campbell, David Perry, Abednigo Inman, William Horner, William Conway, Michael Rawlings, Andrew Greer, William McCormack, Samuel Brashiers, William Armstrong, John Kerr and Landon Carter who were Elected tried and Sworn the truth to Speak upon the Issue Join'd upon their Oath do say That the Defendant is Guilty of the Trespass alledged against him in manner and form as charged in the bill of Indictment Therefore it is considered by the Court that the said James Gooden be amerced (p 341) in the sum of Ten pounds to the use and behoof of the people of this State, together with the Costs expended in the prosecution of this Suit for which he may be taken.

STATE OF NORTH CAROLINA------plaintiff)
      against   (Indicted for a Trespass
WILLIAM WYAT----------------------Defendant)

                     The Defendant being Charged upon the bill of Indictment and asked whether he was Guilty of the Trespass alledged therein against him, Saith that he is not Guilty, and of this he puts himself upon the Country and William Cocke Esquire Attorney for the State doth the same likewise, whereupon Came a Jury (towit) John Hanner, George Pearce, Robert Campbell, Major Temple, John Strain, Thomas Gibbons, Arthur Galbrath, Benjamin Holland, Joseph Crouch, William Hughes, David Wright and Christopher Acoff, who were elected tried and Sworn the truth to speak upon the Issue Joined upon their Oath do say, That the Defendant is Guilty in manner and form as charged in the bill of Indictment, Therefore it is considered by the Court that the Defendant William Wyat, be amerced in the sum of Ten Pounds Currency to the use and behoof of the people of this State, and that he pay the Costs in this prosecution expended for which he may be taken.

STATE of NORTH CAROLINA- plaintiff)
      against   (Indicted for a Trespass.
GALOP CARTER---------------Defendant)

The Defendant being charged upon the bill of Indictment and asked whether he was guilty of the Trespass therein alledged against him saith That he is not Guilty and of this he put himself upon the Country, and William Cocke Esquire Attorney for the State doth the Same likewise, whereupon a Jury was awarded (towit) James Campbell, David Perry, Abednigo Inman, William Horner, William Conway, Michael Rawlings Andrew Greer, William McCormack, Samuel Brashiers, William Armstrong, John Kerr and Landon Carter, who were elected tried and (p 342) sworn the truth to speak upon the Issue Joined, upon their Oath do say that the Defendant Calop Carter is Guilty of the Trespass alledged against him in manner and form as Charged in the bill of Indictment. Therefore it is Considered by the Court that the above Defendant Calop Carter be amerced in the Sum of Twenty five pounds to the use and behoof of the people of this State and that he pay the Costs expended in the prosecution of this Traverse, for which he may be taken.

STATE of NORTH CAROLINA-- plaintiff)
      against   (Indicted for Horse Stealing.
THOMAS GOING ------------ Defendant)

The Defendant being arraigned and Charged upon the bill of Indictment and appeared therein against him for plea saith that he is not guilty of the felony and Horse stealing and puts himself upon the Country & William Cocke Esquire Attorney for the State doth the same where upon Came the following Jury to wit, John Strain, Major Temple, Arthur Gilbrath, John Stone, Landon Carter, James Lea, Benja. Holland, James Campbell, James Hill, John Ker, Wm McCormack, and David Perry who were elected tried and sworn the truth to speak upon the issue Joined upon their Oaths do say that the Defendant Thomas Going is not guilty of the fellony and Horse Stealing in manner and form as charged in the bill of Indictment. Therefore it is Conjectured by the Court that the said Thomas Going be forthwith discharged upon his paying the expense of this prosecution for which he may be taken

Ordered that Court be adjourned untill tomorrow nine O'clock.

(p 343)   August 1790

Friday Morning 20th August
  Court met according to adjournment.

STATE of NORTH CAROLINA - plaintiff)
      against   (Convicted for Horse Stealing
ELIAS PYBORNE------------ Defendant)

Being called to the bar and being asked if he had any thing to say why sentence according to law should not be passed upon him saith nothing. It is therefore Ordered that the said Elias Pyborne be confined in the public pillory one Hour; That he have both his Ears nailed to the pillory and sevred from his head that he receive at the public whipping post Thirty nine lashes well laid on and be branded on the right cheek with the letter H and on his left cheek with the letter T and that the Sheriff of Washington County put this sentence into Execution between the hours of twelve and two this day.

STATE of NORTH CAROLINA)
     against   (Indicted for Horse Stealing
EZEKIEL ABELL   )

                  The Defendant being arranged and charged upon the
bill of Indictment and asked whether he was guilty of the Felony and Horse
Stealing therein charged against him saith, That he is not guilty and of
this puts himself upon the Country and Wm Cocke Esquire attorney for the
State doth the same whereupon this day came a Jury who were elected tried
and sworn the truth to speak upon the Issue Joined upon their oaths do say
that the defendant is guilty of the Felony and Horse stealing in manner
and form as Charged in the bill of Indictment whereupon the defendant by
his attorney moves for a new trial and for reasons appearing to the Court
that the same may be granted whereupon a Jury is awarded to wit, Major
Temple, Robert Campbell, John Strain, Wm Hughes, (p 344) Absdnigo Inman,
Wm McCormack, Michl Rawlings, Andrew Greer, Samuel Brasshires, William Conway, William Armstrong, John Stone, who were elected tried and sworn the
truth to speak upon the Issue Joined upon their oaths do say that the Defendant is not guilty in manner and form as Charged in the bill of Indictment.

            Therefore it is considered by the Court that the defendant Ezekial Abell
be forthwith discharged upon his paying the Costs expended in this prosecution for which he may be taken.

Present the Honorable,
        David Campbell)Esquires
          and   (Judges
        John McNairy) Who each of them did produce a commission from
                            under the hand of George Washington Esquire
President of the United States appointing them Judges in the territory and
authorizing them to hold the said Court upon which certificate there was
certificate Under the hand of William Blount Esquire Governor that the said
Judges had taken the oath to support the Constitution of the United States
and also an Oath of Office.

Francis Alexander Ramsey appeared and produced a Commission under the hand
of William Blount Esquire Governor appointing the said Ramsey Clerk of said
Court upon which there was a certificate under the hand of David Campbell
Esquire Judge certifying that the said Clerk had taken oath to support the
Constitution of the U. S. and also an oath of office. (p 345) and said
Francis Ramsey entered into Bond with Josiah Love, Alexander Outlaw and
William Clark his securities in the penal sum of Two thousand dollars con-
ditioned for the faithful discharge of the duties of his office.

Ordered that Court be adjourned until tomorrow morning ten Oclock.

Monday 1798 25th day of February Court met according to adjournment.

GEORGE GILLESPIE---Plft)
    against   (Debt in the Deteneet
JAMES HUBBARD--Defendant)

The Defendant by James Reed Esquire his attorney came and defends the Wrong & when where & for pleas saith that he hath made payment of the debt in the declaration supposed and of this he put himself upon the Country, and the plaintiff likewise and now this day came the parties by their Attorneys and thereupon came a Jury towit, John Arnwine, John Yancy, John Bergan(Fergan) Thomas Nenient, John Caywood, Wm McCormack, William Hughes, Joseph Brittain, Robert Lane(Love), Charles Robertson, Joshua Kelley, and John Campbell, who were elected tried and sworn the truth to speak upon the issue Joined upon their oath do say that defendant hath not payed as in pleading he hath alledged and that they assess the plaintiffs damages by reason thereof to thirty nine pounds twelve shilling and nine pence besides his Cost. Therefore it is Considered by the Court that the plaintiff recover against the Defendant his damages aforesaid in form aforesaid assessed together with his Costs by him in this behalf Expended and the Defendant in Mercy.

(p 346) STATE of TENNESSEE)
WASHINGTON COUNTY) I Jacob Leab Clerk of the County Court of Washington County hereby certify that the foregoing transcript of the Early records of said County is substantially Correct. It being impossible to make a perfect transcript of said Records in consequence of the mutilated condition of many parts of same and illegible Character and condition of the writing therein.

Witness my hand and seal this the 15th day of Oct. 1887.

Jacob Leab
County Court Clerk

-A-

AARONVIN [SIC]
JOHN, 30
AARONWINE
JNO., 20
JOHN, 4, 7, 14, 25,
29, 30
ABELL
EZEKIEL, 121, 125
ACOFF
CHRISTOPHER, 119,
121, 123
TIMOTHY, 75, 101,
102, 103, 104,
105, 106
ADAIR
JOHN, 4, 7, 14, 20,
25, 54, 57, 60,
64, 67, 72, 77,
84, 90, 92, 96
ADAMS
JOHN, 47, 49, 87
JOHN, JR., 71
JOHN, SR., 71
ROBERT, 47, 49
ADDIR (ADAIR)
JOHN, 97
ALEXANDER
JOHN, 95, 96, 97,
98, 99
ALEXR.
L.S., 6
ALISON
ROBERT, 82, 87
ALLEN
ROBERT, 87, 101
ALLISON
DAVID, 80, 86, 91,
120
JAMES, 121
JOHN, 61, 64
ROBERT, 34, 61, 64,
89, 90
AMIS
LUCY, 83
THOMAS, 16, 23, 27,
32, 35, 44, 47,
51, 55, 59, 62,
66, 70, 76
AMISS
THOMAS, 90, 91
ANDERSON
JAMES, 54
JOHN, 38, 95
JOSEPH, 6, 12, 19,
20, 22, 24, 29,
30, 34, 35, 36,
41, 45, 50
ARMSTRONG
LANTY, 110
LAUGHTR [SIC], 110
MARTIN, 44, 48, 51,
55, 59, 69
WILLIAM, 97, 112,
115, 117, 118,
119, 120, 121,
122, 123, 124,
125
WILLIAM, JR., 110
WILLIAM, SR., 110,
111, 116
ARNOLD
JOHN, 92
ARNWINE
JOHN, 126

ARRANWINE
JOHN, 103, 104
ASHERST
WILLIAM, 35
ASHERT
WILLIAM, 16, 23, 27,
32
AUSTIN
NATHAIEL [SIC], 107
NATHANIEL, 101, 102,
103
AVERY
W., 93
WAIGHTSELL, 117
WAIGHTSTILL, 96, 97,
100, 102, 104,
119, 121, 122

-B-

BAILEY
COTTERAL, 44, 48,
51, 55, 62, 66,
76, 83
COTTRAL, 59, 71
BAIN
ALEXANDER, 55, 59,
62, 66, 71, 76
BAINE
ALEXANDER, 48, 52,
76, 83, 101
BAKER
ELIJAH, 111
ELISHA, 90, 91, 110,
113, 114, 117
BALCH
HEZEKIAH, 120, 121
BARNET
JAMES, 48
BATES
THOMAS, 25, 26
BATTS
THOMAS, 39
BAUGHAN
SAMUEL, 3
BAUGHMAN
SAMUEL, 8
BAYLESS
JOHN, 82
BEALOR
JACOB, 94, 96
BEAN
EDMOND, 55, 60
EDMUND, 48, 52
JESSE, 39
RUSSELL, 96, 97, 98
BEARD
EZEKIEL, 88, 89
JOHN, 30, 31, 34, 69
BELER
JOHN, 18
BELFOR
ANDREW, 114
BELL
WILLIAM, 112
BERRY
FRANCIS, 90, 94, 96
JAMES, 44, 47, 51,
55, 59, 62, 66,
70, 76, 83
THOMAS, 10, 18, 38,
44, 101, 102,
103, 104, 105,
106, 119
THOS., 50
WILLIAM, 44
BISHOP

JOSEPH, 54
BLACKBOURNE
JOHN, 110
BLACKBURN
ARCHIBALD, 26, 87
ROBERT, 93
BLAIR
JOHN, 9, 30, 100,
101, 103, 104,
105, 106
JOSEPH, 81, 87
BLAKE
PETER, 118, 119
BLEVENS
WILLIAM, 27
BLEVINS
ARMSTEAD, 105,
119
DILLEN, 31, 39, 90,
94
JOHN, 61, 64, 68,
72, 78, 84, 95
WILLIAM, 3, 8, 9,
12, 13, 15, 19,
20, 21, 37, 38,
39, 41
BLOUNT
WILLIAM, 1, 6, 19,
29, 38, 125
BOOTH
DAVID, 33, 36, 43,
51
BOOTHE
DAVID, 17, 24, 28,
47, 54, 58, 62,
65, 70, 75, 76
BOUNDS
JESSE, 25, 26
BRAG
DAVID, 119
BRAGG
DAVID, 119
BRASHIER
SAMUEL, 120
BRASHIERS
SAMUEL, 119, 121,
123, 124
BRASSHIRES
SAMUEL, 125
BRINDLE
RICHARD, 7
BRINDLEE
RICHARD, 112
BRITTAIN
JOSEPH, 30, 31, 45,
110, 119, 126
BRITTON
JOSEPH, 9
BROMLEY
AUGUSTINE, 26
BROWN
JACOB, 75
JOHN, 3, 8, 13, 20,
39, 41
RUTH, 5, 49, 52, 56,
60, 63, 67, 71,
77, 83
BRUMLEY
AUGUSTINE, 9, 16,
22, 31, 35
BRYANT
JAMES, 12, 17
BUCHANAN
JOHN, 14
BUCKNER
WILLIAM, 117, 118
BULL

JOHN, 5, 11, 12
BULLAR
ISAAC, 112
BULLARD
ISAAC, 6
JOSEPH, 12, 17
BULLER
ISAAC, 111
BULLOCK
LEONARD H., 2, 9, 15
BUNDIE
SIMON, 109
BUNDY
SIMON, 92, 96
BURK
WILLIAM, 68
BURKE
WILLIAM, 73, 78, 79,
85
BURLESON
AARON, 26
BURLISON
AARON, 25

-C-

CAGE
WILLIAM, 114
CALAHAN
EDWARD, 102
CALBOCK
HENRY, 94
CALDWELL
ANDREW, 122
BENONI, 68, 73, 78,
85
DAVID, 26
CALLAHAM
EDWARD, 89
CALLAHAN
EDWARD, 103
CAMPBELL
DAVID, 1, 6, 12, 19,
20, 22, 24, 29,
34, 35, 36, 38,
41, 45, 64, 69,
74, 81, 88, 89,
90, 91, 95, 100,
109, 118, 125
JAMES, 119, 120,
121, 122, 123,
124
JOHN, 89, 91, 95,
110, 111, 112,
113, 115, 116,
117, 118, 126
ROBERT, 54, 101, 110,
118, 119, 120,
121, 123, 125
WILLIAM, 14
CARMICHAEL
JAMES, 110, 111,
112, 113, 114,
116, 117
CARNEY
JOHN, 16, 23, 34,
37, 43, 46, 50,
54, 58, 62, 65,
70, 75, 82, 109
CARRICK
MOSES, 64, 68, 73,
78, 85
CARSON
DANIEL, 103
DAVID, 95, 100, 101,
103, 104, 105,
106, 107

JOHN, 63
MOSES, 95, 96, 97, 98, 99
CARTER
CALEB, 7, 12
CALOP, 123, 124
EDMUND, 102
JOHN, 38, 39, 57, 71
LANDON, 9, 19, 29, 71, 74, 100, 102, 103, 104, 105, 106, 110, 115, 120, 122, 123, 124
LANTON, 95
CASWELL
DAVID, 25
MARTIN, 4, 7, 8, 9, 11, 13, 18
RICHARD, 81, 87
WILLIAM, 81, 87
CAWOOD
JOHN, 47, 51
CAYWOOD
JOHN, 96, 103, 104, 105, 111, 113, 114, 116, 117, 118, 126
JOHN, SR., 94, 96, 101, 110, 119
CHAMBERS
HENRY, 88, 89
CHARTERS
JAMES, 56, 63, 67
JOHN, 60
CHESTER
WILLIAM P., 74, 80
CHOAT
AUSTIN, 50
CHOTE
MARY, 103
CHRISTIAN
GILBERT, 13
CHRISTMAS
WILLIAM, 68, 73, 78, 79, 85
CLAIBORN
WILLIAM CHARLES COLE, 53, 57
CLAIBORNE
WILLIAM CHARLES COLE, 61
CLARK
WILLIAM, 125
CLOUD
JASON, 114, 115
CLOWER
JOHN, 49, 52
COBB
ARTHUR, 104
BENJAMIN, 89, 98, 102, 103
PHARIOH, 91
PHAROAH, 9, 119
WILLIAM, 47, 49, 52, 56, 60, 63, 67, 71, 84, 95, 98, 99
COCKE
WILLIAM, 19, 26, 28, 33, 36, 40, 42, 46, 50, 54, 58, 61, 65, 69, 74, 82, 91, 97, 100, 103, 106, 107, 113, 114, 115, 116, 117, 120,

122, 123, 124
WM., 125
COILE
ROBERT, 73
COLLUM
DANIEL, 106
COLYER
JOHN, 98, 120
CONWAY
GEORGE, 47, 49, 56
HENRY, 9, 29, 33, 95, 96, 118, 119
JOSEPH, 9, 90, 91, 101, 118, 120
THOMAS, 93, 94
WILLIAM, 9, 47, 49, 52, 56, 60, 63, 67, 71, 77, 84, 118, 120, 121, 122, 123, 124, 125
COOPER
ELIJAH, 89, 90
ROBERT, 97
COULTER
JOHN, 79, 86
COULTON
JOHN, 73
COWAN
ROBERT, 94, 96
COX
JOHN, 14, 90
JOHN, JR., 16, 23, 27, 32, 35
JOHN, SR., 16, 23, 27, 32, 35
JOSHUA, 72
WILLIAM, 9, 16, 22, 26, 31, 35, 49, 77, 89, 90, 98, 100, 101, 102, 103, 104, 105, 106, 107
CRAFT
MICHAEL, 110
CRAIG
ROBERT, 17, 23, 28, 33, 61, 64, 68, 72
CRINDER
JOHN, 45
CRINER
JOHN, 47
CROCKET
ANDREW, 110, 111, 112, 113, 114, 118
CROCKETT
ANDREW, 114, 116, 117
CROUCH
JOSEPH, 45, 82, 119, 121, 123
CULBIRTH
BENJAMIN, 81
CURREY
SAMUEL, 90, 91, 93

-D-

DAHERTY
PETER, 93
DANIEL
JAMES, 81, 87
DAVIS
JAMES, 91
NATHAN, 121

NATHANIEL, 34, 56, 60, 63, 67, 114
DEADERICK
DAVID, 74, 108, 109
DELANEY
WILLIAM, 96
DELANY
WILLIAM, 94, 95
DELLINGHAM
RACHEL, 3
VACHEL [SIC], 8
DEN
JOHN, 104, 114
DENN
JOHN, 94, 103, 105, 106, 111
DENTON
ABRAHAM, 90, 91
JAMES, 91
DILLINGHAM
RACHEL, 3
DOHERTY
GEORGE, 25, 90, 91, 110
PETER, 92
DOLPHIN
WILLIAM, 116
DOLY
AZARIAH, 49
DONALSON
STOCKLEY, 60
DONELSON
STOCKLEY, 46, 49, 52, 53, 56, 63, 67
STOKELY, 72
DOTSON
ELIZABETH, 81
DOUGHERTY
GEORGE, 26
DUM
JOHN, 93
DUNCAN
ANDREW, 110, 111, 112
JOHN, 101, 102, 103, 104, 105, 106, 107, 108, 119
JOSHUA, 88, 92
DUNKAM
JOHN, 3
DUNLAP
EPHRAIM, 24, 28, 33, 37, 40, 43, 46, 50, 54, 58, 69, 75, 82
EPHRAIM M., 34
RPHRAIM, 42
DUNLOP
EPHRAIM, 61, 62, 65, 70, 75
DUNWOODY
ADAM, 90, 101, 103, 104, 105, 106, 107, 108
SAMUEL, 101

-E-

EARNEST
HENRY, 90, 91, 101
EASLEY
ROBERT, 110
EASLY
ROBERT, 110
EDDEN
JAMES, 92

EDEN
JAMES, 109
EDENS
JAMES, 96
EKLES
BENJAMIN, 3
ELLIOT
THOMAS, 95
EMERT
ANDREW, 64
JACOB, 64
ENGLISH
ANDREW, 2, 5, 9, 11, 15, 21, 26, 31, 49, 106
ERWIN
BENJAMIN, 61
EDWARD, 61
JOSEPH, 97
ERWINE
BENJAMIN, 57, 63, 67, 72, 77, 84
EDWARD, 57, 63, 67, 72, 77, 84
EVANS
JESSEE, 47, 49, 71
JOHN B., 80
WILLIAM, 45, 47, 56, 60, 63, 67, 101
EVENS
JOHN B., 86

-F-

FAGAN
JOHN, 13, 48
FAIN
EBENEZER, 91
RICHARD, 93
FEAGAN
JOHN, 44
FEGAN
JOHN, 22, 27, 32, 49, 52, 55, 60
FEN
RICHARD, 103, 105, 111, 114
FENN
RICHARD, 94, 104, 105, 106, 111, 114
FERGUSON
JOHN, 121
FERQAN (FERGAN)
JOHN, 126
FINE
PETER, 110, 111, 113, 114, 117
FITZGERALD
GANETT, 17
GARRET, 36, 58, 65, 70, 75
GARRETT, 24, 28, 43, 47, 51, 54, 62
FOO
NICHOLAS, 93
FORD
BENJAMIN, 17, 24, 28, 33, 36, 43, 47, 51, 58, 62, 65, 70, 75, 76
JOSEPH, 97
FORDS
BENJAMIN, 54
FOWLER
JOHN, 12, 14
FULSOM

JAMES, 115, 116
FULSON
  JAMES, 115

-G-

GAINES
  JAMES, 45
GAINS
  JAMES, 47, 69
GALBRAITH
  ARTHUR, 95, 97, 119,
    121, 122, 123
GALBREATH
  ARTHUR, 121
  JAMES, 75, 83
  JAS., 8
GAMMON
  RICHARD, 110
GARDENER
  WILLIAM, 58
GARDINER
  WILLIAM, 29, 34, 46,
    70
GARDNER
  WILLIAM, 36, 41, 43,
    50, 54, 62, 65,
    75, 82
GASS
  JOHN, 101, 118, 119
  JOSEPH, 101
GEST
  BEN., 59
  BENJAMIN, 52, 55,
    63, 66, 71, 76,
    101
GIBBONS
  THOMAS, 80, 86, 119,
    120, 121, 123
GILBRATH
  ARTHUR, 124
GILLALAND
  JOHN, 33, 36
GILLASPIE
  THOMAS, 26
GILLENWATER
  JOEL, 85
GILLENWATERS
  JOEL, 30, 31, 68,
    73, 78
GILLESPIE
  GEO., 38
  GEORGE, 125
GILLILAND
  JOHN, 24, 29, 37,
    43, 47, 49
GILLISPIE
  GEORGE, 105
GIST
  BENJAMIN, 48, 83,
    101, 103, 104,
    105, 106
  JOHN, 90, 91
  JOSEPH, 95
  JOSHUA, 90, 91, 110,
    111, 113, 115,
    117
GITZGERALD [SIC]
  GARRETT, 33
GOING
  THOMAS, 124
GOODEN
  ALEXANDER, 122
  BENJAMIN, 113
  JAMES, 123
GOODIN
  BENJAMIN, 113

GOODWIN
  ALEXANDER, 12
  BENJAMIN, 5, 11, 12
GORDON
  JOHN, 101, 102, 103,
    104, 105, 106
GORSORCH
  JOHN, 119, 120
GOSSARCH
  JOHN, 94
GOSSCORCH [SIC]
  JOHN, 96
GRANTHAM
  RICHARD, 110
GRAY
  AGNESS, 92, 114
GREENE
  JOSHUA, 91
GREENLEE
  JAMES, 49, 53
GREER
  ALEXANDER, 54
  ALEXD., 34
  ANDREW, 31, 44, 48,
    51, 54, 55, 59,
    69, 70, 71, 75,
    76, 83, 95, 99,
    100, 102, 103,
    104, 105, 106,
    108, 120, 121,
    122, 123, 124,
    125
  ANDREW, SR., 44, 47,
    51, 55, 59, 62,
    66
  JAS., 15
  JOSEPH, 4, 5, 8, 95,
    100, 101, 102,
    103, 104, 105,
    106
GWIN
  ROBERT, 44

-H-

HACKET
  JOHN, 37
HACKETT
  JOHN, 4, 43, 46
HADIN
  JOSEPH, 18
HALL
  JOHN, 68, 73, 78, 85
  WILLIAM, 91
HAMILTON
  ALEXANDER, 5, 8, 14,
    22, 27, 32, 35,
    39
HAMLEN
  DANIEL, 82
HAMLIN
  DANIEL, 96, 97, 98
  DAVID, 95
HAMLTON
  ALEXANIER [SIC], 1
HAMMER
  JOHN, 89, 90, 95,
    96, 98, 99, 100,
    101, 110, 111,
    112, 113, 115,
    116, 117, 119,
    120, 123
HANNAH
  JOHN, 2, 5, 8, 10,
    15, 21, 26, 37
HARDEN
  BENJAMIN, 113

JOSEPH, 110, 111, 113,
  114, 117, 121
JOSEPH, JR., 118
JOSEPH, SR., 100,
  118, 119
HARDIN
  JOSEPH, 31
HARKLERHODE
  HENRY, 64
HARRIS
  SAMUEL, 4, 7, 14,
    19, 20, 25, 26,
    30, 31, 41, 45,
    50, 53, 57
  STEPHEN, 25, 26
HARRISON
  MICHAEL, 53, 56, 60,
    63, 67, 72, 77,
    84, 95, 100, 109,
    110, 116, 119
  SAMUEL, 39
HARRISS
  SAMUEL, 93, 103, 104
HART
  DAVID, 2, 9, 14
  NATHANIEL, 2, 9, 15
  THOMAS, 2, 9
HAUGHTON
  THOMAS, 73
HAWKINS
  NICHOLAS, 74, 79, 86
HAWTHORN
  NOAH, 95
HAY
  JAMES, 75
HAYES
  CHARLES, 39, 45, 53,
    57, 104
HAYGOOD
  JAMES, 54
HAYS
  CHARLES, 4, 7, 14,
    19, 20, 25, 26,
    30, 31, 41, 50
HEARD
  SAMUEL, 115
HENDERSON
  A., 2
  COLO., 32
  ELIZABETH, 2
  JOHN, 2
  NATHANIEL, 46, 49,
    52, 68, 73, 97
  NATHL., 78, 79, 85
  RICHARD, 2, 9, 15,
    28, 33, 36, 40,
    42, 46, 50, 54,
    58, 61, 65, 69,
    74, 82
  SAML., 78, 85
  SAMUEL, 68, 73, 79
  THOMAS, 25, 34
  THOS., 50
HENDERSON & CO., 21, 26,
  31, 35, 39, 42,
  45, 50, 53, 57,
  61, 64, 69, 74,
  81
HERRITAGE
  JOHN, 4, 7, 8, 11,
    13, 18, 20, 25
HICKS
  ISAAC, 90
HILL
  DANIEL, 112
  JAMES, 101, 103,
    104, 105, 106,

    107, 108, 118,
    119, 120, 121,
    122, 123, 124
HODGE
  FRANCIS, 64
HOGG
  JAMES, 2, 9, 14
HOLLAND
  BENJA., 124
  BENJAMIN, 82, 119,
    120, 121, 122,
    123
HONLEY
  SAMUEL, 30
HOOD
  ROBERT, 34, 36, 41,
    43
HORN
  LAURENCE, 80
  LAWRENCE, 86
HORNER
  WILLIAM, 9, 118,
    120, 121, 122,
    123, 124
HOSKENS
  JESSE, 118
HOSKINS
  JESSEE, 9, 119
  NINIAN, 92
HOUGHTON
  THOMAS, 79, 86
HOUSTON
  JAMES, 12, 17
  ROBERT, 44
HOWARD
  JOHN, 107
HUBBARD
  JAMES, 125
HUBBART
  JAMES, 91
HUBBERT
  JAMES, 40, 90
HUES
  WILLIAM, 91
HUGHES
  DAVID, 15, 22, 93
  ELIZABETH, 87, 88
  FRANCIS, 110
  THOMAS, 75
  WILLIAM, 87, 88,
    119, 120, 121,
    122, 126
  WM., 125
HUGHS
  DAVID, 3, 5, 8
  WILLIAM, 123
HUMPHREYS
  MOSES, 16
  MOSSES [SIC], 23
HUNT
  JOHN, 73, 89, 93,
    95, 101, 109, 110
HUNTER
  JOHN, 91
HUTCHINGS
  THOMAS, 25, 26, 29,
    33

-I-

INGLE
  GEORGE, 56, 60, 63,
    67, 72, 77, 84
INGLISH [SIC]
  ANDREW, 34
INGRAM
  THOMAS, 85

WILLIAM, 73, 79
INMAN
  ABEDINGO, 89
  ABEDNIGO, 91, 95,
    96, 97, 98, 99,
    110, 119, 121,
    122, 123, 124,
    125
  SHADRACH, 101, 103,
    104, 105, 106,
    107
  WILLIAM SHADRACH,
    101
IRVINE
  ROBERT, 98
IRWIN
  WILLIAM, 49, 53
ISAAC
  ELIJAH, 93

-J-

JACKSON
  ANDREW, 74, 81
  SAML., 86
  SAMUEL, 80
  THOMAS, 74
JATHAM [SIC]
  HOWEL, 61
JERVIS
  EDWARD, 108
  JAMES, 111
JOAB
  JACOB, 90
JOBB
  JACOB, 91
JOHNSON
  JOHN, 73
  WALTER, 54
JOHNSTON
  JOHN, 64, 68, 78, 85
  WALTER, 29, 30, 31
  WILLIAM, 2, 9, 15
JONES
  JOHN, 34
  JOHN LETTEN, 48
  JOHN LETTON, 48, 51,
    55, 59
JUGAN
  JOHN, 35

-K-

KALBOCK
  HENRY, 94
KEER
  ROBERT, 58, 62, 65,
    70, 75, 83
KELLEY
  JOSHUA, 89, 90, 126
KENNEDAY
  DANIEL, 101
KENNEDY
  DANIEL, 101
KERKYNDOLL
  SIMON, 7, 10
KERR
  DAVID, 95
  JOHN, 121, 122, 123,
    124
  JOHN, SR., 119
  ROBERT, 16, 23, 27,
    32, 37, 43, 46,
    51, 54
KETTERING
  LAURENCE, 51
  LAWRENCE, 44

KETTERON
  LAWRENCE, 59
KETTERRING (KETRON?)
  LAURENCE, 47
KETTRON
  LAURENCE, 66, 70
  LAWRENCE, 62
  SAMUEL, 54
KEYWOOD
  JOHN, 44, 54, 59,
    62, 66, 70, 105,
    106, 107, 108
KILE
  ROBERT, 79, 85
KINCADE
  DAVID, 54
KING
  JAMES, 80
  JOHN, 97, 101, 114
  ROBERT, 40
  THOMAS, 68, 73, 78,
    81, 85, 87, 88
KIRKENDOL
  SIMON, 4
KIRKENDOLL
  SIMON, 18
KUYKENDOLL
  JAMES, 99
KUYKINDOLL
  JAMES, 99

-L-

LAMBERT
  DANIEL, 94, 96
LANE (LOVE)
  ROBERT, 126
LARKENS
  DAVID, 111
  HENRY SAMPSON, 112
LARKIN
  DAVID, 34
LARKINS
  DAVID, 108, 110
LAUGHLIN
  ALEXANDER, 95
  JOHN, 17, 23, 28,
    33, 61, 64, 68,
    72, 96, 101, 102,
    103, 104, 105,
    106, 107, 108
  JOHN, SR., 94
LEA
  JAMES, 101, 103, 104,
    105, 106, 107,
    118, 119, 120,
    122, 124
  SAMUEL, 108
LEAB
  JACOB, 126
LEETNAL
  JOHN, 2
LEWES
  BENJAMIN, 120, 121
  HANAH, 120
  HANNAH, 121
LEWIS
  ANDREW, 48
  JOHN, 92
LONG
  JOHN, 13
LOONEY
  BEN, 58
  BENJAMIN, 29, 34,
    36, 41, 43, 46,
    50, 54, 62, 65,
    70, 75, 82

  DAVID, 95, 96, 97,
    98, 99, 101, 104
  ELIZABETH, 92, 114
  MANY, 29
  MARY, 34, 36, 41,
    43, 46, 50, 54,
    58, 62, 65, 70,
    75, 82
  MICHAEL, 112
LOVE
  JOSEPH, 6
  JOSIAH, 6, 125
  ROBERT, 89, 90, 100,
    101
LOYD
  JOHN, 111
LUTTERAL
  JOHN, 9
LUTTERALL
  JOHN, 15

-M-

McAFEE
  ROBERT, 4, 18
McAFFEE
  ROBERT, 7, 10
McCALL
  PETER, 13, 22, 27,
    32, 35, 44
  ROBERT, 95, 96, 97,
    98
McCAUL
  PETER, 92
McCHALLON
  ABRAHAM, 13
McCLELLAND
  ABRAHAM, 101, 120
  ABRAM, 102, 103,
    104, 105, 106,
    107, 108, 119,
    122
  ALEXANDER, 119
McCLENAHAN
  [BLANK], 71, 76
McCLENIHAN
  WILLIAM, 48
McCLOUD
  WILLIAM, 119
McCOMACK
  WILLIAM, 101
McCORD
  JAMES, 110
McCORKLE
  JOSEPH, 114
  SAMUEL, 90
McCORMACK
  WILLIAM, 49, 95, 109,
    110, 119, 120,
    121, 122, 123,
    124
  WM., 125, 126
McCOY
  ABRAHAM, 90, 91
  ANANIAS, 26
McCRAE
  CHARLES, 45
McCUBBIN
  ZACHARIAH, 119
McCUSTON
  BENJAMIN, 107, 108
McDOWEL
  JOHN, 49
McDOWELL
  ANN, 63
  CHARLES, 4, 7, 8,
    11, 13, 18, 20,

    25
  JOHN, 5, 52, 56, 60,
    63, 67, 71, 77,
    83
McFARLAN
  ALEXANDER, 36
McFARLAND
  ALEXANDER, 34, 41,
    43
McGUIRE
  [BLANK], 92, 93
McKAY
  JOHN, 32
McMINN
  JOSEPH, 77, 84, 95,
    96, 97, 98, 99
McNABB
  DAVID, 71
  JOHN, 90, 91, 101,
    102, 103, 104,
    105, 106
McNAIR
  JAMES, 101, 102,
    104, 105, 106
McNAIREE
  PETER, 44
McNAIREY
  JOHN, 90
McNAIRY
  JOHN, 1, 6, 12, 38,
    45, 53, 57, 114,
    121, 125
McNAMEE
  PETER, 44, 110
McNUTT
  GEORGE, 25, 26
MACOY
  FANNY, 2
  SYRICE, 2
  SYRUCE, 2
McPETERS
  DAVID, 4, 7, 8, 11,
    13, 18, 20, 25
McPHETERS
  SAMUEL, 97
MAHAN
  JAMES, 101
MAHON
  DAVID, 94
MAJORS
  STEPHEN, 94, 96
MARTIN
  GEORGE, 2, 5, 9, 11,
    15, 21, 26, 31,
    34, 49, 106
MASSINGAL
  HENRY, 3, 5, 8, 15
MASSINGALE
  HENRY, 22
MATTHEWS
  ALEXANDER, 89, 90
MAXWELL
  GEORGE, 13, 114
MAY
  SAMUEL, SR., 56, 60,
    63, 67, 72, 77,
    84
MEDLOCK
  WILLIAM, 45, 47
MEEK
  ADAM, 26
  ALEXANDER, 16, 23,
    27, 32, 37, 43,
    46, 51, 54, 58,
    62, 65, 70, 75,
    83
MELIGEN

JOHN, 31
MELIKEN
JOHN, 30
MESSER
NICHOLAS, 106
MILIKEN
JOHN, 73, 78, 79, 85
MILLER
HENRY, 93
JOHN, 110
MILLIGAN
JOHN, 100, 101
MILLIKEN
JOHN, 69
MITCHEL
GEORGE, 16
RICH., 1
MITCHELL
GEORGE, 23, 102,
109, 114, 120
MARK, 80, 86, 105
MARY, 114
RICHARD, 73, 79, 82,
85
ROBERT, 86
MOFFIT
ALEXANDER, 99,
119(2), 122
MOFFITT
ALEXANDER, 98
MONTGOMERY
HUGH, 49
JAMES, 95, 100, 101,
103, 104, 105,
106, 107, 108
MICHAEL, 44, 47, 51,
55, 59, 62, 66,
68, 70, 73, 75,
78, 79, 80, 85,
86
MOORE
ANN, 43, 50, 51, 54,
58, 62, 65, 70,
75, 82
ANNE, 34, 37
GEORGE, 44
WILLIAM, 96, 97
MORRIS
JAMES, 47
JOHN, 45
SHADRACH, 98
MORRISON
PETER, 95
MORRISS
SHADRACH, 95, 98, 99
MORRISSON
PETER, 96
MORROW
WILLIAM, 95, 118,
119
MURPHEY
WILLIAM, 53, 56, 60,
63, 67, 72, 77,
84
MURPHY
JOHN, 110
MURR
RICHARD, 110
MURREL
RICHARD, 114
MURRELL
RICHARD, 111, 112,
113, 116, 117,
118

-N-

NASH
WILLIAM, 95, 114
NcNAIRY
JOHN, 121
NEILSON
WILLIAM, 113
NELSON
ALEXANDER, 54, 88
HENRY, 95, 110, 111,
112, 113, 115,
116, 117, 118
JOHN, 26
WILLIAM, 2, 5, 8, 10,
15, 21, 26, 37,
89, 90, 91, 93,
110, 111, 112,
113, 114, 116,
117, 118
NENIENT [SIC]
THOMAS, 126
NEWMAN
JOHN, 82, 90, 93,
95, 96, 97, 98,
99, 101, 103,
107, 108, 110,
118, 119
NORTH
PHILIP, 88
NOWLAND
GEORGE, 54
JOHN, 91

-O-

ODELL
JOB, 122
OLDHAM
HENRY, 56, 60, 63,
67, 72, 77, 84
NANCY, 56, 60, 63,
67, 72, 77, 84
OOULTER (POULTER?)
JOHN, 46
OUTLAW
ALEXANDER, 4, 7, 8,
11, 12, 13, 17,
18, 20, 25, 90,
91, 95, 101, 103,
104, 105, 106,
118, 119, 125
OVERTON
JOHN, 80

-P-

PAIN
JESSEE, 75
PARKISON
PETER, 93
PATTERSON
JAMES, 1, 5, 8, 16,
22, 27, 32, 35,
39
JOHN, 25
JOOHN, 26
ROBERT, 7, 14, 17,
22, 27, 32, 35,
40, 42, 45, 50,
53, 57, 61, 65,
69, 74, 81
ROBT., 6
WILLIAM, 50
PAYNE
THOMAS, 3
PEARCE
GEORGE, 110, 111,
113, 114, 117,

118, 119, 120,
121, 123
PEMBERTON
JOHN, 94, 96, 101,
105, 110
WILLIAM, 105
PERIMON
BINONE, 34
PERKINS
NICHOLAS, 25
PERRY
DANIEL, 95
DAVID, 101, 119,
120, 121, 122,
123, 124
PICKENS
JAMES, 113, 114
PIG
RICHARD, 120
PITNER
JOHN, 87
POWER
JOHN M.U., 50
PRATER
THOMAS, 82
PRESTON
COLLO., 14
PRITCHET
JOHN, 48, 52
PRITCHETT
JOHN, 55, 60
PRITHEROW
ALEXANDER, 90, 91
PUGH
JONATHAN, 92, 96,
109
SUSANNAH, 96, 109
PURSELLY
WILLIAM, 110
PY COURNE [SIC]
ELIAS, 122
PY COWINE [SIC]
ELIAS, 122
PYBORNE
ELIAS, 124

-R-

RADER
ADAM, 122
RAMSEY
F.A., 8
FRANCIS A., 5, 15,
19, 109
FRANCIS ALEXANDER,
8, 39, 88, 125
RANKEN
DAVID, 110
RANKIN
DAVID, 90, 91, 110
RANNALS
JOSEPH, 37
RAWLINGS
ASAHAL, 110
ASAHEL, 25, 111,
113, 115, 117,
118
DANIEL, 76, 83
MICHAEL, 30, 118,
120, 121, 122,
123, 124
MICHL., 125
RAYGAN
CORNELIUS, 110, 111
REASE
JAMES, 105
REASONER

GARRETT, 119
REED
JAMES, 38, 74, 86,
87, 126
JOHN, 80
REES
DAVID, 36, 42
JAMES, 91
REESE
DAVID, 24, 28, 33,
40, 54
JAMES, 113
RENNALDS
JOSEPH, 43
RENOLDS
JOSEPH, 46
RHEA
JOHN, 6, 56
JOSEPH, 119
M., 69
WILLIAM, 90
RHODES
CHRISTIAN, 102
RICE
JOHN, 54
RICHARDSON
JAMES, 37, 89, 93,
95, 100, 109, 118
RICHEY
MARGARET, 93
ROACH
JORDAN, 37, 38
ROAN
ARCHIBALD, 19, 37,
43, 46, 53, 57,
61, 64
ROANE
ARCHIBALD, 69, 74,
81
ROBERTSON
CHARLES, 126
ROBINSON
CHARLES, 18, 37, 38
ROBISON
CHARLES, 110, 111,
113, 114, 115,
117
ROCK
[BLANK], 92, 93
RODDYE
JAMES, 74
RODGERS
JAMES, 90
ROBERT, 87, 89, 90
THOMAS, 26, 87
ROGERS
JAMES, 91
ROBERT, 114
THOMAS, 95, 96, 97,
98, 99
ROLLINGS
ASAHEL, 9
ROSE
HOSEA, 93
ROWAN
ARCHIBALD, 90, 91
RUSSELL
ANDREW, 1, 6
DAVID, 34, 82, 90,
91, 93, 95, 101,
110, 111, 113,
115, 117, 118,
119
GEORGE, 74
LEWIS, 74
WILLIAM, 81, 87
RUSSILL

132

ANDREW, 6
RUTLAND
  ISAAC, 5
RUTLEDGE
  GEORGE, 89, 93, 94,
    118
  ROBERT, 45
RUTLEGE
  GEORGE, 49
RUTLIGE
  ROBERT, 47
RYAN
  JAMES, 47

-S-

SAMMONS
  GEORGE, 3
SAUNDERS
  MARY, 24, 28
  PHILIP, 17, 24, 28
SCOTT
  JOHN, 27, 49, 95,
    96, 97, 98, 99
  WILLIAM, 110
SCROGGS
  EBENEZER, 91
SEVIER
  JAMES, 30, 31, 43
  JOHN, 9, 18, 45, 94
  JOHN, JR., 80, 86,
    93, 94, 102
  ROBERT, 17, 18
  VALENTINE, 104
SHARP
  JOHN, 57, 60, 64,
    67, 72, 77, 84,
    94
  WILLIAM, 90
SHARPE
  JOHN, 96
  WILLIAM, 21, 91, 94,
    110, 114, 118,
    119, 120
SHELBY
  EVAN, 13, 14
  ISAAC, 87
  JOHN, 3, 4, 7, 9,
    12, 14, 15, 18,
    19, 21, 22, 25,
    27, 29, 30, 37,
    38, 41, 64, 68,
    72, 78, 84, 103
  JOHN, SR., 61
  T., 69
SHELTON
  JOHN, 54, 55
SHIELDS
  JOHN, 53, 56, 60,
    63, 67, 72
  PATRICK, 106
SHIRLEY
  JOHN, 24, 29, 33,
    37, 43, 47, 49
SHOAT
  AUSTIN, 24, 28, 33,
    40, 42, 46, 54,
    58, 61, 65, 69,
    75
  AUSTON, 36, 82
SHULTZ
  CHRISTIAN, 91, 93,
    103
SIMS
  JOHN, 47
SITZREAVES
  JOHN, 18

SKILLERN
  WILLIAM, 74, 79, 86
SLAVES
  BET, 75
  CLAYBOURNE, 120
SMALL
  WILLIAM, 108
SMITH
  DANL., 19
  EZEKIEL, 21
  JOHN, 69, 73, 78,
    79, 85, 88
  SAMUEL, 17, 24, 28,
    95, 105
SOOMAN
  JACOB, 87
SPENCER
  SAMUEL, 90, 91
STANLEY
  JOHN HENRY, 53
STEPHENSON
  WILLIAM, 100
STERLING
  EDMUND, 96
  EDWARD, 94
STEVENSON
  WILLIAM, 101
STEWART
  DAVID, 74
STINSON
  JAMES, 6, 49
STOCKTON
  JOSHUA, 73
STONE
  JOHN, 95, 118, 121,
    124, 125
STRAIN
  JOHN, 30, 45, 89, 91,
    95, 96, 97, 98,
    99, 110, 119,
    122, 123, 124,
    125
STRIPLING
  CLAYTON, 99, 122
  THOMAS, 99
STUART
  DAVID, 80, 107
  JAMES, 3, 5, 8, 15,
    22, 88, 89, 90,
    94, 100, 110
  ROBERT, 18
STUBBLEFIELD
  WYAT, 10
SUMMERS
  JOHN, 92
  SIMON, 92

-T-

TADLOCK
  JOHN, 5, 6, 111,
    112, 116, 117
TALBOT
  MATTHEW, 16, 23
TAPACOT
  JAMES, 71
TAPSCOT
  JAMES, 76
TATE
  JOHN, 116
TATHAM
  HOWELL, 64
TAYLOR
  CHRISTOPHER, 75, 93
  ISAAC, 90, 91
  LEEROY, 34
  NATHANIEL, 71

NATHL., 81
THOMAS, 97
TEMPLE
  MAJOR, 90, 91, 101,
    118, 119, 120,
    121, 122, 123,
    124, 125
THOMAS
  ISAAC, 53, 56, 60,
    63, 67, 72, 77,
    84
TIGH
  JOHN, 33, 36
TIPTON
  ISAAC, 82
  JOHN, 88, 89, 90,
    96, 100, 101,
    103, 104, 105,
    106, 107, 108,
    109, 110, 111,
    112, 115, 116,
    118, 119
  JOHN, JR., 122
  JOHN, SR., 119
  JONATHAN, 91
  JOSEPH, 100
  THOMAS, 121
TITSWORTH
  THOMAS, 101, 102,
    103, 104, 105,
    106, 107, 108
TOOL
  JOHN, 37, 43, 46
  RUTH, 37, 43, 46
TOPP
  ROGER, 17
TORBETT
  AGNES, 68, 73
  AGNESS, 78, 79, 85
  ALEXANDER, 68, 73,
    78, 79, 85
TREMBLE
  WILLIAM, 9
TRIMBLE
  WILLIAM, 100
TRUESETT
  CHRISTIAN, 90
TRUXWELL
  CHRISTIAN, 90
TURNEY
  PETER, 17, 18
TYE
  JOHN, 24, 28, 40, 42

-U-

UMSTEAD
  JOHN, 2
  SUSANNA, 2

-V-

VANCE
  JOHN, 17, 23, 28,
    33, 61, 64, 68,
    72, 101
  SAMUEL, 69
VAUGHTER
  JESSE, 94, 96
  PHILEMON, 94, 96
VAUTER
  JESSE, 90
VINCENT
  GEO., 69
  GEORGE, 3, 25, 45,
    47, 110, 111,
    113, 114, 117,

118
THOMAS, 31
VINCIENT
  GEORGE, 26
  THOMAS, 30

-W-

WADDEL
  JOHN, 6, 7, 16, 17,
    97
WADDELL
  JOHN, 22, 27, 61, 69
WADDILL
  JOHN, 40, 45, 50,
    53, 57, 65
WADDLE
  JOHN, 32, 34, 35,
    42, 54, 74, 81,
    97
WALDEN
  E., 10
  ELISHA, 10, 12, 16,
    18, 23, 27, 32
WALDON
  ELISHA, 36
WALLEN
  ELISHA, 40, 42, 45,
    50, 53
  ELISHAL [SIC], 47
  JOHN, 54
WALTON
  JUDGE, 86
WASHINGTON
  GEORGE, 125
WEAR
  JOHN, 30, 31, 82,
    89, 91, 95
WEIR
  JOHN, 54
WESTFALL
  ABEL, 105
WHARTON
  WILLIAM, 102
WHITCRAFT
  JOHN, 90
WHITE
  ISAAC, 75
  JAMES, 25, 32
  RICHARD, 89
WHITSON
  WILLIAM, 63, 71
WIDENER
  LEWIS, 90, 91
  LUCES, 97
WILLIAMS
  EDMOND, 20, 25, 97,
    99, 102
  EDMUND, 4, 7, 14,
    89, 90, 92, 96
  JAMES, 44
  JOHN, 2, 9, 14, 74
WILLSON
  JOHN, 64
  SAMUEL, 10, 32, 36,
    40, 42, 44, 45,
    53
WILSON
  ALEXANDER, 90
  JOHN, 113, 114, 116
  JOSEPH, 117, 118
  SAMUEL, 10, 12, 16,
    18, 23, 25, 27,
    45, 46, 47, 50,
    75, 101, 117, 118
  WILLIAM, 92, 117,
    118

WOOD
  BALT, 83
  BAT, 71
  BATT, 52, 55, 59,
    60, 63, 66, 76
  HENRY, 3
  JOHN, 8, 48, 52, 55,
    60
  RICHARD, 111, 113,
    117, 118, 119
  SAMUEL, 82
  THOMAS, 52, 55, 63,
    66, 71, 76, 83
  THOS., 59
WOODS
  BALT, 48
  BATT, 48
  JOHN, 3
  RICHARD, 48, 52, 55,
    59, 63, 66, 71,
    76, 83, 110, 115,
    118
  THOMAS, 48
WORLEY
  DAVID, 94
WRIGHT
  DANIEL, 110
  DAVID, 48, 52, 55,
    59, 62, 66, 71,
    76, 83, 111, 112,
    113, 114, 116,
    117, 118, 119,
    120, 121, 122,
    123
WYAT
  WILLIAM, 123

-Y-

YANCEY
  JOHN, 110
YANCY
  JOHN, 74, 80, 86,
    111, 112, 113,
    114, 116, 117,
    118, 126
YOUNG
  JOHN, 114
  JOSEPH, 54, 75
  ROBERT, 93